FOUL DEEDS & SUSPICIOUS DEATHS
IN & AROUND LEICESTER

FOUL DEEDS AND SUSPICIOUS DEATHS Series

Wharncliffe's *Foul Deeds and Suspicious Deaths* series explores, in detail, crimes of passion, brutal murders and foul misdemeanours from early modern times to the present day. Victorian street crime, mysterious deaths and modern murder tell tales where passion, jealousy and social depravation brought unexpected violence to those involved. From unexplained death and suicide to murder and manslaughter, the books provide a fascinating insight into the lives of both victims and perpetrators as well as society as a whole.

Other titles in the series

Please contact us via any of the methods below for more information or a catalogue.
WHARNCLIFFE BOOKS
47 Church Street – Barnsley – South Yorkshire S70 2AS
Tel: 01226 734555 – 734222; Fax: 01226 724438
E-mail: enquiries@pen-and-sword.co.uk
Website: www.wharncliffebooks.co.uk

Foul Deeds & Suspicious Deaths In & Around
LEICESTER

KEVIN TURTON

Wharncliffe Books

First Published in Great Britain in 2005 by
Wharncliffe Books
an imprint of
Pen and Sword Books Ltd.
47 Church Street
Barnsley
South Yorkshire
S70 2AS

Copyright © Kevin Turton 2005

ISBN: 1-903425-75-1

Typeset in 11/13pt Plantin by Concept, Huddersfield.

Printed and bound in England by
CPI UK.

Pen and Sword Books Ltd incorporates the Imprints of
Pen & Sword Aviation, Pen & Sword Maritime,
Pen & Sword Military, Wharncliffe Books,
Pen & Sword Select, Pen and Sword Military Classics
and Leo Cooper.

For a complete list of Pen & Sword titles please contact
PEN & SWORD BOOKS LIMITED
47 Church Street
Barnsley
South Yorkshire
S70 2BR
England
E-mail: enquiries@pen-and-sword.co.uk
Website: www.pen-and-sword.co.uk

Contents

Introduction

... the shocking horror of murder in all its grisly guises.

From the early days of the nineteenth century, as books and newspapers became increasingly available to an ever greater number of people, accounts of murder and suspicious death began to capture the imagination of the public at large. So passionate were they about the subject, most writers and reporters quickly realised that whenever a crime of this nature occurred they had almost free license to report on the circumstances in a depth of detail previously unheard of. Regardless of the ability of their readers to understand the text, illiteracy being high, they knew the literate were all too well prepared to read aloud in pubs, clubs and meeting rooms to any that would listen. This in turn gave them a wider audience than they had been hitherto able to reach and also allowed them a degree of economy when it came to telling the truth. From this came the single printed broadsheets announcing the arrest of the killer, which were widely circulated and, if found guilty at their trial, the killer's final condemned cell confession detailing their life. These so-called confessions were often sold to the huge crowds that flocked to see an execution.

For the Victorian public, detailed true life crime reportage was often mimicked by lurid and sensational fictional stories loosely based around fact, known as *Penny Bloods*. These were always strikingly illustrated, eight pages long and packed with vivid tales of murder and mayhem. They sold in their thousands and attracted a readership drawn to the shocking horror of murder in all its grisly guises. As the nineteenth century progressed and education improved, this same readership became more discerning. The popularity of the old broadsheets as a method of dissemination when it came to murder slowly declined, as did the sensationalism portrayed by the artists and writers of the *Penny Bloods*, who found it increasingly difficult to maintain their grip on the public imagination. Literacy had spread across the country with every passing year and with it a level of discernment that had not existed when they first picked up their pens. The same public that had once bought so enthusiastically and recoiled in mock horror at the murderous detail these men had produced, no longer found it germane to their life or their lifestyle. Greater knowledge, improved living conditions and the ability to read, had shifted the public's perception of most things criminal. From the fiction writer they demanded a level of honesty and plausibility in the stories they told and from the reporter they insisted on both accuracy and truth. The fiction writer quickly adapted and by the end of Victoria's reign so had the newspapermen. In the case of the latter it was their ability to translate the drama of the courtroom into a piece of prose that won them their readership. The ability, in a similar way to that of the novelist, to express not only the horror behind the detail but also of the pressures and emotions experienced by all those involved in a trial, virtually ensured they also held on to it. So true crime was born and there can be no doubting our continued fascination with the subject.

In *Foul Deeds and Suspicious Deaths in and Around Leicester* I have used this same principle and put together a comprehensive case study of the crimes that dominated the city over the past hundred years or so. Crimes whose stories eclipsed all other news of the day, capturing the headlines of not just local news-papers but in many cases those of the national press. These were read avidly by Leicester's public at large and not just because of the nature of the crime, which was murder, but also because of the gladiatorial atmosphere of the courtrooms in which those accused were brought to account. One must remember, of course, that to be found guilty in all the cases I discuss meant a death sentence.

Also included here amongst the list of the notorious are some of Leicester's most baffling and still unsolved murders such as the utterly perplexing death of James Gray Lowe and, of course, the now world famous and equally mysterious, *Green Bicycle Murder*. These two cases alone merit an in-depth study and invite the reader today, as they did many years ago, to attempt to unravel a mystery that has confounded countless would-be sleuths and curious authors. Each of the following pages is, therefore, a glimpse into a not too distant past that will both shock and fascinate.

So, please enjoy the journey and as you do so may I also take a moment to thank all those at the Record Office at Leicester whose help and guidance often goes unnoticed. I would also like to thank the *Leicester Mercury* and all those newspaper-men that over a century and more reported diligently on all things important to the people of Leicester, and whose almost verbatim reportage of the activities of the Leicester courthouse have been of great assistance. Lastly, I must offer up a huge thank you to Maureen Yule whose patience has been boundless and whose photographic skill has once again proved invaluable.

CHAPTER 1

The Price of Envy
The Murder of Acres Fowkes
1855

... William saw a sudden movement outside the window ...

ohn Fowkes had been born into a comparatively wealthy family but, it could be argued, had never benefited from that wealth. His father, known to have walked a fine line where the law was concerned, had inherited the one hundred acre farm at Snareston, including a number of cottages, long before he had been born. Believed to have been a Resurrectionist before that inheritance came about, he had been suspected for years of having stolen and sold freshly buried corpses to various dubious medical establishments in Birmingham. The notion that he would have embraced farming in the manner he did had surprised most that knew him. Not only had he taken to the life, he had done so spectacularly, proving himself surprisingly successful in all aspects of agriculture, and turning himself into an astute businessman. The wealth he accumulated, however, was never to be spent on the education of his children.

John was the eldest of three brothers and two sisters, none of whom had received anything other than a simple, rudimentary schooling and, as he grew older, he began to resent that omission from his childhood. Always known by the nickname of 'butcher' by any that knew him in the village on account of having taken up the trade as a young man, he had initially tended to work from premises in the village. But by the mid 1840s, possibly still feeling somewhat embittered, he had enlisted in the army and moved away from Leicestershire. It

The small village of Snareston today. The author

did not last long. After serving with his regiment in Ireland he began to make overtures toward his father for money. Disaffected by military life, and quite probably unable to accept the discipline it also demanded, he made the decision that the lesser of the two evils was home and family.

By 1855 he was back on the farm working alongside his younger brother, William. As a farm labourer his sense of discontent was ever stronger, as by now he believed his station in life to have been thoroughly usurped by his own nephew. His father, now an old man, may have helped him escape the army but was never going to allow either himself or his brother any form of responsibility or control over the farm. Instead, he had, over the latter years of his life, invested money in his daughter Elizabeth's son, Acres Fowkes. Whether because age had brought with it a realisation that none of his own family would be capable of taking over the farm on his death, or simply that he regretted his refusal to educate his sons effectively when he had had the opportunity, he never explained. Either way his nephew was the beneficiary of good schooling for much of his life and at its conclusion had then been brought, with his mother, to live in the farmhouse and take full business control of the farm. As the year drew to a close Acres responsibility had even been widened, not only to control the farm's business accounts but also to oversee much of the day-to-day running, which meant he had, in all but name, become the overall farm manager. This power enabled him to manage the labour force and with it the daily working lives of his two uncles. Incensed by all he saw John refused to live in the same house and moved into a farm cottage some half

From an Edwardian postcard. Author's collection

a mile away. Bitterly resentful, he made no secret of his growing hatred for the young man and most of the villagers knew he harboured sentiments that were both serious and dangerous. In fact they helped fuel them. On 25 November of that same year John was told, by a man he knew well, that Acres had taken £700 from his father. John wanted to know why.

With that aim in mind he had stormed into the cowsheds early that evening in search of his brother William and, when he finally found him, he demanded to know if the rumour was true. Whether William could possibly have known is extremely doubtful but in an attempt to calm his brother he told him that he believed the sum of money that had been given over was only £100. It did little to assuage John's anger and he swore vengeance for what he believed was an injustice committed by his father. He told William he would put an end to Acres involvement in the farm and leaving him to cogitate on exactly what he meant by that he stormed off toward his own house.

That same night, whilst all this was taking place, Acres Fowkes was sitting in the *Square and Compass* public house drinking with the village policeman, PC Cooper. The two men had known each other for several years and were considered friends, and when the landlord shouted time he invited the constable back to the farmhouse for another drink. Not one to refuse hospitality, PC Cooper readily accepted and the two arrived back at a little after 11 pm. William was already in the house having laid out fresh straw for the cattle. His father, who suffered badly from asthma, was standing at the open kitchen window trying to suck in fresh air. The three men were familiar with his symptoms, which did not cause them too much concern and they left him where he stood. Acres suggested they all have a drink and after drawing beer from a cask kept in the

The Globe, *once the* Square and Compass. The author

kitchen each pulled up a chair and sat by the fire. At about the same time William saw a sudden movement outside the window where his father stood and gave a startled shout, 'There's Butcher!' Everyone turned to look and as they did so the glass pane shattered. There was a gunshot and Acres Fowkes instantly fell backwards from his chair wounded in the head. PC Cooper was the first to react and ran toward the door. He found his exit barred from the outside by means of a length of wood, which had been passed through the door latch handle and securely tied to a post beside the house's back wall. It took several minutes for he and William to cut through the rope and by the time they had succeeded in reaching the farmyard, John Fowkes had fled. Whether through shock or uncertainty the young constable made no attempt to follow the killer. Instead, he organised someone to fetch Spencer Edmonds, surgeon, from Appleby whilst he returned to Snareston where he despatched another constable to Ashby de la Zouch to fetch sergeant John Platts.

Platts, for obvious reasons, took some time to arrive and it was after 4.30 am when he finally walked into the Snareston police house. By this time Acres Fowkes had been attended by the doctor and had fallen into a coma with no chance of recovery. But the police sergeant, unlike his constable, was a meticulous man when it came to viewing a crime scene. After examining the ground outside the window from where the shot was fired, he discovered a number of distinctive footprints. These he followed for much of the length of the field that stretched out beyond the farm until they disappeared around an opening in the hedge. The piece of land on the other side formed part of a narrow road, the surface too compacted to show any further prints. Certain that whoever had fired the gun had run along this road the sergeant followed a hunch. Ducking under the hedgerow he followed the contours of the narrow track until it entered into another open field. There, in the glare of his lamp, the footsteps reappeared and travelled for several yards towards another narrow road. Here they finally petered out but not until they were within sight of Fowkes farm cottage. Platts knocked at the door and to his surprise the knock was answered. John Fowkes appeared not to have been in bed, dressed as if he were about to go off to work. He told the sergeant he had been up since 2 am and vigorously denied having been up at the farm and showed the policeman a gun, which he claimed was the only gun he possessed and one that had been broken for some time. After a cursory examination the sergeant, somewhat unconvinced, believed it had been fired and quite possibly only hours earlier. He duly arrested Fowkes. Platts also took the gun, some shot he found in the house and, of course, Fowkes's boots. These were to prove crucial.

Four days after the arrest Acres Fowkes died and the original police charge of wounding was changed to one of murder. Despite strong denials it was William's identification of his brother as being the man he had seen outside the kitchen window that brought John to trial, but it was John's own boots that helped prove his guilt. When Platts had followed the footprints through the fields he had seen that one of the boot prints, that of the right boot, had a distinctive mark on the sole. The leather had been somehow cut causing a clear indentation. The boots Fowkes had worn at his arrest matched the prints the police sergeant had followed. When he stood in the dock before Lord Chief Justice Campbell at 9 am on the morning of 8 March 1856, he must have realised just how perilous his

St Bartholomew's Church, Snareston. The author

situation was. Throughout his three-month incarceration he had stoically stuck to his story that he had not fired the shot that killed Acres.

It was to make little difference. Not even brother William's valiant attempt at discrediting his own statement of events, telling the court from the witness box that he was no longer certain, had any impact. Prosecution counsel gently coaxed him through his evidence, no doubt all too well aware of his difficulty, until he was forced to acknowledge that he had clearly seen the face of the man that fired the gun. Once admitted, any ambiguity as far as identification was stripped away. He could not have had so clear a sight and not have been able to identify his own brother had it not been his face at the window, or so ran the prosecution argument and William was forced to confirm his eyewitness evidence had been accurate. It was damning stuff and when added to the fact that John only owned one pair of boots it condemned him to death.

At eight o'clock on the morning of 19 March he made the short walk to the scaffold erected before the County Gaol surrounded by a huge crowd that had been gathering since the previous evening. All the windows of houses and businesses along Carlton Place had been boarded up to protect them from damage should the crowd begin to riot. There was no need. John Fowkes made no speech to the mass of eager faces and as William Calcraft placed the noose around his neck a sudden silence fell before the trap opened to launch him into eternity.

CHAPTER 2

For the Sake of a Few Shillings
The Murders of Edward and James Woodcock
1856

... an appalling piece of savagery.

dward Woodcock had lived most of his seventy-nine years in or around Leicester, working generally as a farm labourer. By the end of the 1840s, too old to be involved in manual labour and no doubt all too well aware of his own age and the restrictions it placed upon him, he had moved into the Toll Bar Gate House on the Leicester to Grantham Road, some half a mile outside Melton Mowbray. In need of a house to live in and keen that it be near to his son and his family whose cottage lay only a few hundred yards away, for Edward, the job seemed ready made. Well used to rising early, the life of a gatekeeper, who could be called out at any hour to let travellers pass, held no particular concerns. In fact the job was generally viewed as being particularly suitable for a man of his age because it required little thought and even less energy. Widowed years earlier, Edward had grown used to his own company. This was often a prerequisite for the job because Toll Houses were invariably isolated and loneliness was a part of every day. For many single men it was too much to bear and within months of taking on the job they left. But Edward had no such concerns. He knew there would be few quiet days with a ten-year-old grandson living nearby and so it proved. Young James, like most children of his age, had a keen eye, a curious mind and a lot of time for his grandfather. Most days he made a point of walking to the Toll House so the two could be together but it took some persuading to get him to stay the night. Used to being close to other houses he always felt nervous as night fell and would insist on walking back home. For some reason he changed his mind only once and it was to prove a fatal decision.

At around two-thirty on the morning of 19 June 1856 a man named William Brown gave the familiar shout of 'Gate' from the road that brought Edward from his bed. Still in his nightshirt, and probably recognising the voice of a man he had met two days earlier, he pulled open the front door expecting to receive the penny payment from a man on foot. Instead he was shot once from a pistol, the ball shattering a rib and smashing through his right lung. Brown intended the shot to kill the old gatekeeper instantly and had his aim been a little better it probably would have. But Edward was obviously a man of great strength and despite the appalling wound he managed to grab a hold of Brown as he attempted to gain entry to the house. The two fell backward through the open door and after a fierce fight during which the old man sustained savage knife wounds to his hands and chest, he was unceremoniously dumped on the floor and left to die. Probably at that point Brown realised that there was someone else in the house. No doubt frightened out of his wits, young James, who had heard all that had taken place from

The Leicester to Grantham Road today. The author

the adjoining bedroom, hid himself beneath the bedclothes. Brown simply hunted him down, stabbed him in the groin, ripped open his stomach and then slit his throat. It was an appalling piece of savagery.

The bodies lay undisturbed until 4.30 am when an agitated Alfred Routen, en route to Grantham to deliver his bread, had been forced to leave his cart on the road. After receiving no response to his repeated shouts he went in search of the gatekeeper. Edward Woodcock was clearly dead. In the light of a June dawn the baker could see from the state of the mutilated corpse and amount of blood splattered about the room that there was no chance he had survived the attack. Unaware of the grandson laid in the next room, Routen did the obvious, ran from the house and rode his cart to the village of Thorpe. There he roused local constable, John Clayton, from his bed and in company with one or two other villagers retraced his journey back to the house. By mid-morning, Leicester's Superintendent Condon was on the scene and immediately set up a door-to-door enquiry searching for any new faces in the neighbourhood over the previous few days.

In a community where strangers were rare and people travelled little it was hardly surprising that the name of William Brown suddenly came to the forefront. Born in Melton

Melton Mowbray. The author

Mowbray, he hardly fit the profile of stranger. But Brown, *Peppermint Billy* as everyone knew him, had only returned back to Melton Mowbray in May after serving thirteen years as a transported convict in Australia and that made him a stranger. Numerous sightings were recorded from people claiming to have seen him in the area throughout much of the previous week, including one from a farmer who claimed Brown had told him that the old gatekeeper had refused him a glass of water. Other sightings from a variety of locals also put him in the area of the Toll House only two days earlier. Despite the lack of any substantial evidence it was enough for the Superintendent and a manhunt was launched.

Only too well aware of what the police would do after the discovery of the murders Brown had made for the north of England, no doubt confident that if he could put enough distance between himself and the law he could possibly escape. After skirting the villages of Holwell, Broughton and Plumptree, he arrived in Nottingham at around two o'clock that same afternoon where he was seen boarding a train to Leeds. By the following day he was in Wetherby. But the net was already closing in. Police had issued a circular to every police station across Yorkshire and also given a reasonably accurate description to the Yorkshire newspapers for their weekend editions. If Brown had managed to stay away from populated areas for a few days then quite possibly he would never have been caught. But Brown can hardly be described as being bright. On Sunday 22 June he walked into a Primitive Methodist Chapel, made a show of himself by refusing to remove his hat or take a seat, which drew obvious attention and then followed some of the congregation into the nearby *Blacksmith's Arms*. Having caused a furore amongst the church-going folk it was hardly likely he was not going to be discussed and that in turn caused the landlord, a Mr Mason, to ask him one or two pertinent questions about just where he had arrived from. With an accent that was out of place amongst the local dialect the questions seemed reasonable to ask. Brown, for his part, had no difficulty in answering. What he did have difficulty with was consistency. He failed to answer some of the questions accurately enough, and by now suspicious, the landlord re-read a description of the Toll House murderer he remembered reading earlier that day in a Leeds newspaper. Recognising in that description the man he now saw sitting in his bar he immediately sent out for the police. But Brown, unaware of what was taking place around him, calmly drank up and left. Fortunately for Police Constable Eccles he did not wander far. Some hundred yards or so from the pub he sat on a fence to talk to some children and there he remained until the policeman was able to make the arrest.

On the following day he was put on a train along with a strong police escort and returned to Leicester. Such was the anger of local people who had been primed to expect his arrival by local newspaper reports, that when his train pulled in to Leicester railway station he was met by a screaming mob intent on their own justice. William Brown would have ended his life there had it not been for the huge police presence that succeeded in keeping the crowds at bay whilst they manhandled him out of the station and on to a cart that took him to Leicester prison. He made a brief court appearance on the following day during which he pleaded not guilty. After a second hearing on 24 June he was ordered to stand trial for murder.

The trial itself opened on 14 July before Lord Chief Justice Jervis. William Brown, according to the *Leicester Advertiser*, conveyed an unexpected sense of confidence from his place in the dock. Quite possibly he had good reason to believe that he would be found not guilty. He must have known that murder was going to be extremely difficult to prove. There was no concrete evidence in existence that could either place him at the scene, or back up police contention that he wielded the weapons that had caused the two deaths.

Immediately after the discovery of the bodies a search of the Toll House had revealed two items. One was the pistol that fired the shot, which had been carelessly discarded by the killer inside the house; the other a small item known as a tobacco stopper. The pistol had been easily identified as being one of the murder weapons because it fired a two-ounce ball. The ball that had passed through Edward Woodcock had been found and fit the bill neatly. After examination by an expert it was also confirmed that it was the type of gun rarely found in this country but in popular use in the colonies. The tobacco stopper, which was apparently a common item and therefore harder to place, had apparently been seen by a watchmaker who claimed in court that he had seen William Brown pull this out of his pocket amongst loose change whilst in his shop some three days before the murders.

Of the two items only the pistol, or at least one very similar in type, could be argued by the prosecution to have been in Brown's possession with certainty. After his arrival back from the Australian penal colony William Brown had paid a visit to his brother, John. The two had apparently argued over John's wife, Anne. It appeared William had met his sister-in-law on several occasions since his return and, consumed by jealousy, John had accused the two of sleeping together. Whether or not they had is not known but William, despite his brother's accusations, did disappear with her for several days. When the two finally turned up again William was brandishing a pistol, which by his own admission was of an unusual type. This was not positively identified as being the same as the one found at the murder scene, although it apparently matched it in appearance. Witnesses brought to court claiming to have seen William during the days running up to the murders never saw him armed, neither did any of his clothing reveal blood staining despite the certain knowledge that whoever murdered the Woodcocks had used a knife and, in the case of the old man, that knife had been wielded whilst involved in a fight.

In his summing up to the jury the judge highlighted these specific facts and told them to proceed with care:

> . . . *With regard to the identity of the pistol and the tobacco stopper the evidence is not of that conclusive character that it should be in order to justify them returning an adverse verdict. It appeared from the evidence that the prisoner was near to the place where the murder was committed, some short time previously he had made some silly enquiries about the old man; that he talked about the old man refusing him a glass of water. But would they for one moment believe that the fact of him refusing him a drink of water could have induced the prisoner to go to the old man's house in the dead of the night, and take away his life?*

He went on to re-affirm the defence claim that all the evidence presented had been circumstantial and that nothing existed in evidence that could with certainty place him at the scene of the crime. Clearly for the judge there were serious doubts.

Not so the jurors. Probably swayed by the argument that guilty men don't run away they returned a verdict of guilty. Certainly there was enough evidence to support that verdict, conjectural as it was. There was no doubting that Brown had been in the vicinity of the Toll House at least two days prior to the killings and that he had met the old man. Also that at some point in the run up to the murders he had owned a pistol. If that pistol had been of common type possibly no one would have remembered much of it but it was not and, for William Brown, perhaps more than any other fact, this one reinforced the guilty verdict.

A petition was mounted within days in an attempt to force a reprieve on the grounds of insanity. It had no chance of success. The question of William Brown's mental condition had never been raised at his trial and the Secretary of State refused to entertain the notion. The execution took place before a large crowd on 25 July 1856 with Brown approaching the scaffold calmly, still insisting that he was innocent.

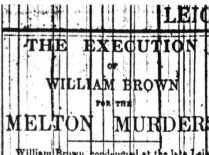

Newspaper headline of William Brown's execution.
Leicester Advertiser

CHAPTER 3

An Unfortunate Secret
The Murder of Emma Green
1876

...John Green had intended to murder his wife ...

When John Thomas Green married Emma, the love of his life, in 1856, she was pregnant with their first child. Over the next twenty years it was a 'state of health' she was to grow accustomed to, giving birth to nine children. This in turn meant they moved house more than once in search of greater space until finally they arrived at 40 Lee Street, Leicester, at some time in the 1860s. With more rooms available for the family to use and with Green employed full-time as a painter in Leicester, the situation seemed to work well for everyone. Certainly not wealthy but, as Emma saw it, able to pay their way without the need of debt, they were reasonably comfortable. John Green was liked by those who knew him and was considered to be a hard-working, honest man who cared deeply for his family. But as the years went by that view became tempered by his increasing dependence on alcohol. A sociable man who, as time went by, spent more and more of his evenings in the nearest pub, though never to the detriment of his work.

Emma never felt financially penalised by his drinking but she did feel brutalised by his temper, which at times could be violent. By 1870 the couple's relationship was in serious difficulty. He appeared to grow ever more disillusioned with the family life he had once embraced so ardently and she resentful of his constant anger. Rows became ever more frequent, neighbours more complaining of the arguments they heard and the children more afraid of their father. By 1874 Green had embarked upon a secret affair. He had met Hannah Davis at some point that year whilst working in Leicester and within days of that meeting was arranging to see her on a regular basis. Hannah living in Loughborough meant these meetings were difficult to set up but somehow he succeeded. Quite probably a deal of the anger he then visited upon his own household was driven by the fact that he desperately wanted to leave Lee Street behind him but knew there was never going to be a way to do that. Emma, with nine mouths to feed, was never going to sanction a split between the two. In the summer of that same year a neighbour, whether well meaning or simply mischievous, told his wife. From that point on life for both of them became intolerable.

It is probably fair to say that by the summer of 1876 John hated Emma with an intensity that would inevitably manifest itself in extreme violence. Taking on a painting job with a gunsmith on Humberstone Gate created an opportunity he seized with both hands. By now desperate to be rid of his wife he fabricated a story around one of his sons needing a gun to shoot birds and asked if a small handgun could be provided for his use. The gunsmith was only too pleased to oblige but set one condition for its payment. If Green accepted the gun then all his work was to be given freely. He agreed and the two men struck a bargain. On 14 August the gun was handed over and after buying a little shot from the workshop Green took the gun home and hid it in the shed at the back of his house. For the next seven days it remained hidden but not out of mind. The arguments escalated to a new and more violent level and Green

Gallowtree Gate, Leicester c.1916. Author's collection

openly began to threaten that he would kill Emma. For her part she refused to take his threats seriously, believing that it was all bluster. Family life went on as normal; only the children it seems registered any real fear. They saw the change and whilst probably never accepting that his threats were very real, they nevertheless realised that something in their father's character had changed. They were right to be fearful.

On Monday 21 August between five and six o'clock in the afternoon Green calmly walked out of the kitchen and walked to his shed. There he picked up the gun, loaded it and returned to where Emma sat beside the kitchen table sewing. From a distance of three feet and without uttering a word he shot her twice in the neck. The first bullet lodged in her spine rendering her completely paralysed, the second lodged at the base of her head. He then walked back out into the yard and sat on a wall. There he stayed until the arrival of police constable Hickinbottom, who made the formal arrest. Emma meantime lingered on in a confused state until 9 am the following morning.

The reason behind the murder being carried out at that particular moment in time was a complete mystery. The couple had just spent a relaxed Sunday with friends and appeared to have patched up their differences; so much so that nothing on the day the killing took place would have suggested a motive. No arguments, no fights and no threats. Green it appeared had cold bloodedly murdered his wife at a time of his own choosing and when it would have been least expected by her or his children. From the moment police made the arrest they knew there was little by way of mitigation and Green initially all too readily acknowledged his guilt. But just a few hours before his wife died he had second thoughts. Perhaps because he suddenly realised the enormity of what he had done he asked to see a police officer and then made a fresh statement. In this revised version of events he claimed that he had not deliberately shot Emma and that the gun had fired accidentally.

The trial opened at Leicester on 1 December that same year before Baron Huddleston. From the outset, the outcome was to be a foregone conclusion. Green, despite his attempt at claiming accidental shooting, was unable to resolve the fact presented by the prosecution that he had loaded the gun with two bullets. This, they argued, showed intent but, they added, to fire off both of those shots proved murder. No one, they insisted, would have accidentally fired a gun twice unless they had meant to do so. When police constable Hickinbottom took the stand before lunch his evidence reinforced this view and effectively condemned Green to the scaffold. He told the court that when initially arrested Green had acknowledged his guilt and told the officer that, 'I am the man'. Aware that Emma was still living at the time of the arrest the young PC then sat him down and charged him with committing grievous bodily harm, the only charge available to him whilst Emma lived. Incensed by what he saw as a lesser crime Green suddenly stood up and questioned the constable's reasoning:

> *Grievous bodily harm, that's all? She dared me to do it and I have done it.*

For the jurors it was irrefutable evidence of guilt. Nothing in the defence team's summing up at the end of the trial was able to surmount this one single fact, that John Green had intended to murder his wife and had accepted his guilt within an hour of carrying out the act. Even the learned judge found it difficult to create any circumstances that would have caused the jurors to

Castle Gateway, Leicester c.1920. Author's collection

return any verdict other than guilty. In his final address he told them clearly not to shirk their duty:

> ... *Learned counsel for the defence had endeavoured to show that it was an accident, and he had also contended that there was no malice, but malice in the eye of the law meant any unlawful act intentionally done. They must consider the intention of the prisoner. If he intended to fire the pistol at her, and death ensued, that was murder. The firing of a pistol loaded with two bullets and in such circumstances was murder. There was no such case made for the defence that the prisoner was not responsible for the act.*

The jury duly obliged and Green was sentenced to death. A petition for a reprieve was quickly raised but rejected by the Home Secretary on 19 December. Green, who had never questioned the court's verdict, had resigned himself to the prospect of execution from the moment he had re-entered his cell. Freely acknowledging his guilt he remained unmoved as the news of the Home Secretary's decision was read to him. He was executed at eight o'clock the following morning.

CHAPTER 4

A Little Box of Secrets
The Murder of Joseph Tugby
1877

He had been savagely beaten about the head.

A hawker by trade, Joseph Tugby was better known around Coalville for the quality of his singing voice. A regular at most public houses in the area, he would often spend his evenings singing to the regulars in return for a night's free ale. But he was also known for something else. Tugby carried two small boxes around with him wherever he went, one a tin biscuit box minus its lid and held together by pieces of string and containing papers and pieces of bone, the other a cigar box whose contents no one ever saw. On the night of 31 August 1877 he walked into the *Stamford and Warrington Arms*, Coalville, carrying his boxes at a little after a quarter past ten at night. He was sober and after exchanging a few pleasantries with landlord William Beckworth, who knew him well, he was joined at the bar by three men. John Upton, James Satchwell and William Swift, all miners from the nearby colliery and known to the landlord, struck up a conversation with Tugby the minute they entered the pub. For the next forty-five minutes this unlikely group of friends stood huddled around the bar deep in conversation ordering up only a single round of drinks before deciding to buy a bottle of whisky before leaving, the cost of which was borne by them all. It was a little after 11 pm and curious as to just where the quartet were going to go at that time of night, particularly with a bottle of Scotch in their hands, Beckworth stood at the door and watched. They did not wander far. At the level crossing, just beyond the end of

The Stamford and Warrington Hotel *today.* The author

the street he saw them cross the road and make for the foot bridge over the railway line that would have taken them on to Hugglescote.

At half past twelve on the morning of 1 September neighbours shouting they had discovered a body awakened police constable George Hardy from his bed. The body was in fact that of Joseph Tugby. He lay just beneath the bottom step of the footbridge and when the young constable found him he was still alive, though unconscious. He had been savagely beaten about the head. So much so that most of his teeth had been knocked out and he lay on the ground where he had slumped into a hunched, sitting position. According to the policeman's later report there was also considerable blood loss:

> *When I first found the deceased the blood was running from his mouth in streams, and ran through the steps: it was flowing on to the embankment in considerable quantities. There were spots of blood on the railings, about eighteen inches above where his head was laying. There were several spots and splashes. The splashes looked as though the man had been beaten.*

He went on to say that he also found a battered and empty biscuit tin at the scene and the lid of a cigar box but nothing

Railway footbridge where Joseph Tugby was murdered. The author

else. Tugby was taken to the Union Workhouse at Ashby de la Zouch where he died a few hours later.

Those living nearest the bridge and who had heard a commotion during the night wasted no time in identifying Satchwell, Upton and Swift as being the men responsible. Despite no one having seen the attack it was enough that all three were well-known in the neighbourhood and had been seen in Tugby's company. In fact there were so many witnesses that all four men had stood drinking together in the bar of the *Stamford and Warrington Arms* and had been seen later at the bridge that their arrest was inevitable. Satchwell and Upton were found later that same day drinking at the nearby *Royal Oak*. Both denied the murder but did accept that they had been on the bridge when the killing took place. Swift, the two argued, had murdered the man in a fit of temper shortly after they had left the *Stamford and Warrington Arms*, but they had not actually witnessed the killing. Tugby, they claimed, had been attacked at one end of the bridge, the opposite end to that upon which they had stood, but at the time they had not realised that Swift had actually killed him. They apparently believed it had been a fracas, no more than that, and as a result he had been pushed down the steps. Unfortunately for the police, whether the story told by the two was truthful or not was unlikely to be verified without Swift in custody, and he had no intentions of being caught. Unlike his two unsuspecting friends he had succeeded in disappearing and evading the intense search made over the days leading up to the inquest.

Joseph Tugby's body was discovered at the foot of these steps. The author

At that inquest, held some four days after the murder at Ashby's Workhouse, evidence was produced by the surgeon who had carried out the post mortem, that proved beyond doubt Tugby had not died as the result of any fall but as the result of extreme violence. The surgeon, William Donovan, told the court that as a direct result of that violence, Tugby had sustained two breaks to his lower jaw, the loss of all his teeth, a fracture over his right eye, a broken nose, a severe wound to his right temple and a fracture of the skull that ran from the left eye to the ear. None of which, he insisted, could be claimed to have been inflicted accidentally. Joseph Tugby had been beaten to death in a most appalling way and also, added the doctor, had he survived would have remained paralysed from the neck down. It was enough for the jury to return a verdict of wilful murder against all three men. Satchwell and Upton, who had been brought to the court at the start of the hearing, realised at that point that they were implicated in the death and no matter how much they pleaded their innocence they needed to offer up stronger evidence in their defence. This they found incredibly difficult to do. Unless Swift was captured and admitted his guilt the two men realised they would stand trial as accomplices to murder. If any further incentive were needed to point the

Once the Royal Oak *where Satchwell and Upton were arrested.* The author

police in the right direction then this was it and they seized the opportunity with both hands. Swift was finally arrested after it became known that there was a secret room in his father's house. A hidden door led from an upstairs room into a loft space. There, well concealed behind a makeshift screen he was found lying in a narrow single bed, hiding beneath a pile of soiled bedding.

But if the other two believed that having delivered Swift to justice that that same justice would suddenly swing into their favour they were to be bitterly disappointed. Swift initially insisted he had not been at the bridge when the murder took place and had hidden away only after he had been told that his two one time friends had implicated him in the killing. In a later statement, perhaps after receiving some legal advice, he had a change of mind and did acknowledge his presence on the bridge at the time Tugby had been attacked. But, he insisted, the attacker had not been he but had been Upton, who he claimed had beaten the man at the top of the bridge steps before hurling him to the ground and kicking him all the way down those steps to the pavement on the Coalville side of the railway line. Furthermore, he added, Satchwell, far from standing passively at the opposite end of the bridge had also taken a role in the beating. All damning stuff but was it enough to save him from the gallows?

The evidence against the three was circumstantial but compelling. All three could be placed at the scene of the crime at the time of the murder but no eyewitness evidence existed that could prove beyond doubt which, if any of them, had actually delivered the beating that killed the hawker. Police inspector Brewitt, who had carried out Swift's arrest, was of the opinion that all three had been involved one way or the other; an opinion reinforced by a late addition to John Upton's original statement. In a letter to police written from his cell he observed that Satchwell had carried a boot in his jacket pocket heavy enough to inflict the type of injuries described in evidence at the inquest. For Brewitt, this added information was simple confirmation that there was an undisclosed fact that all shared. That fact was simply their involvement in murder and the more they argued each had been responsible, the more it began to appear that there was a kind of conspiracy to hide the real truth. Robbery, he believed, was probably the motive. Just what Joseph Tugby had carried around in his little boxes was not known. Some papers, all of no value, had been found on the railway line beneath the bridge, as had the smashed cigar box, but neither revealed exactly what they had contained and by the time of the trial it had become very clear that no one was ever going to know. All three men took their place in the dock and pleaded not guilty and unless any suffered a bout of conscience they would never tell.

The trial, when it started on 5 November, had caused so much excitement across Leicestershire that crowds flocked to the court in the hope of gaining admittance. Too many in fact to be allowed in and the case began with the courtroom packed from wall to wall. For all three prisoners, who no doubt paid little attention to the numbers that packed the public gallery, it was the impact of the first two prosecution witnesses that held their attention. During the intervening weeks since the murder police investigations had succeeded in discovering two witnesses that could place all three at the scene of the murder and at the right time. Reuben Brown and Charles Wain, like the three men in the dock, had been out that night for a drink. As part of their route home both had to cross the bridge at Coalville. According to their testimony they clearly saw Upton, Satchwell and Swift, all of whom they could identify, and another man clutching two boxes, all together at just after midnight. The man with the boxes was of course Joseph Tugby. Whilst it offered nothing by way of evidence proving the three as murderers it did place all four men together some thirty odd minutes prior to constable Hardy being called from his bed. It also helped discredit the statements from Upton and Satchwell claiming that they had left Swift alone on the bridge. When this evidence was corroborated by two other independent witnesses the writing was on the wall.

After two days of conflicting evidence from a variety of witnesses the trial drew to its conclusion and the judge summed up the case for the jury to retire and consider. Theirs, he insisted, was an onerous task when so much evidence had been heard and the three accused

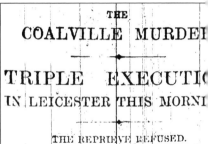

Newspaper headline announcing the triple execution. Leicester Advertiser

had produced conflicting evidence in defence that simply confused their position:

> *If the men went out by a common consent to effect a certain purpose, and death resulted, they were all equally liable. It might be that there was no criminal intent among the prisoners and I, having explained the general propositions of the law, would ask you to apply the facts to it. The prisoners were indicted for the wilful murder of the old man Tugby, and I only wished I could see some reason to doubt that any other person than the prisoners had a hand in his death.*

The jury returned a guilty verdict against all three.

All three were executed in Leicester on 27 November 1877. Whether or not all three were equally responsible no one will now ever know. But as a rider to the case Swift's sister, Clara Matthews, told police shortly after his arrest that her brother had only been married ten weeks when the murder was committed and that had been his first night out alone since his wedding day. Upton and Satchwell had talked him into going out because it had been pay day and all three had arrived back at her house in the early hours of the morning somewhat the worse for wear because of drink. Satchwell, who lodged with her, told her as he washed that on the way back he had beaten an old man with a shoe. As only Upton had ever mentioned the shoe as a weapon could it be that her story was the truth?

CHAPTER 5

The Midland Railway Mystery
The Death of James Gray
Lowe
1886

... Leicester police were totally baffled.

anchester businessman James Gray Lowe spent Friday 20 August 1886 in London. Exactly where he had been is not known but according to friends and some business acquaintances he had travelled south to collect a part payment of a debt. The payment in question was a sum of £1,200, which represented a little over half of a £2,000 debt. Just who owed him the money or who actually paid him is again, not known, but it was thought that the transaction was conducted in cash. Eager to return home he had then bought a first class rail ticket for the 12.01 am Scotch Express from London to Edinburgh and was given fifteen shillings and six-pence in loose change. He was the only occupant of carriage No. 643 and took his seat a few minutes before the train was due to leave. Intent on deterring any fellow passenger from joining him on the journey north, he then pulled down the window blind on the platform side and closed the carriage door. A Mr W. Groves, travelling to Nottingham, noticed the blind as he ran towards the train and not wanting to impose himself on another man's privacy boarded the next carriage along. The train left on time and the journey was uneventful until just after it had passed through Luton station. Mr Groves, who had slept through the journey up until that point, was then rudely awakened by what he later described as a loud crack. Convinced that a stone had been thrown up against the glass of

Leicester Railway Station c.1920. Author's collection

the carriage he jumped to his feet fully expecting to find a hole in the window. There was none. After a few minutes spent running his fingers across the glass surface in search of tell tale signs he convinced himself that he had dreamed the whole event, sat back down and went back to sleep. He was disturbed a second time when the train stopped at Leicester station. Hearing a commotion he opened his carriage door and saw the guard retrieve a gun from the running board beneath the window of the carriage behind. He then watched as the guard opened the carriage door and found James Gray Lowe lying dead with a single bullet through the head. So began the Midland Railway mystery.

After a thorough and careful examination of both the body and the carriage Leicester police were totally baffled. It was clear from the available evidence that James Gray Lowe had been shot. It was also clear that the carriage windows were closed and intact. First impressions suggested that he had committed suicide yet there was insufficient blood staining around the carriage to support the idea, no blood on his clothing and a broken umbrella on the floor. The gun found outside the carriage resting on a footboard that ran the length of every carriage attached to the train yielded up even more baffling clues. It was clear after examination that it had fired the bullet eventually found lodged in the man's temple, but the fact it had remained where it lay, possibly since just north of Luton, seemed impossible. Furthermore the gun was found to have been manufactured in Belgium and was an imitation of an American Smith and Wesson. Upon close examination it was also found to have been fired twice, the first bullet a misfire and still in the chamber; the second the shot that killed. It was also a revolver measuring eight inches in length. This last fact caused great consternation amongst the experts that examined it. A gun of that length used as a weapon of suicide and firing at the angle that caused the wound, meant that the man must have stood up and aimed using his right hand, with the right arm bent toward the head, but inexplicably there were no powder burns to the hair or around the wound.

Leicester's Chief Constable, Mr Duns, in an attempt to clarify this point, had the gun taken to gunsmith and weapons' expert, Henry Clarke. From the back of his shop on Gallowtree Gate, Leicester, a series of tests were then carried out. In order to replicate the wound as best they could whilst at the same time establishing the distance from which the fatal shot had been fired, they used the body of a dead dog. Firing close to the head created a blackening of the fur and a great deal of singeing. From a distance of six inches this same effect occurred but to a much lesser degree. But from a distance of one foot none of these factors occurred, creating an almost perfect replica wound. It appeared on that evidence that the dead man must have been murdered.

However, the Chief Constable was a thorough man. He had the gun returned to the railway station where by this time the carriage had been moved to a secluded shed, and set up a second set of experiments. After a great deal of trial and error it was discovered that if a man opened the window and leaned out of the carriage, held his right arm at an angle with the weapon in his hand, a distance of one foot from the temple area of the head could be achieved. It was also found that if the gun was then dropped there was a reasonable chance that it would strike the running board beneath the window and come to rest on the ledge. According to his later report this happened almost 70 per cent of the time. It was therefore perfectly rational to argue, he believed, that suicide was more than likely. He could not however explain how the window had been closed after the shooting.

At the inquest held at Leicester Town Hall before coroner, George Harrison, these theories were debated at length but found unsatisfactory, particularly after it was shown that a man of James Gray Lowe's size would not have been able to hold the gun any further than six inches from his head. To do so, as was demonstrated, would not have allowed him to pull the trigger with his forefinger. Dr Clifton, who had examined the body, poured more cold water on the theory when he told the court that had the man been standing when the bullet hit him then

The Old Leicester Town Hall c.1890. Author's collection

The Old Town Hall as it looks today. The author

he would certainly have sustained blood staining to his jacket. Holding the coat up in court, he reiterated his original findings on entering the carriage shortly after the body's discovery that no blood had either flowed from or splashed on to it at any point. London police added further confusion when they told the coroner that despite extensive enquiries and after showing the gun to every gun shop owner in the capital they had failed to identify its owner.

By the afternoon of the hearing and in an attempt to produce a solution, the coroner decided that the jury were to be taken to see the carriage. It was his hope that if he allowed them access they could possibly produce a more comprehensive theory than that offered by the experts and one that would perhaps fit more closely with the facts. But on arrival at the railway shed it seemed clear they believed that only one method existed that would offer up any accurate assessment of the facts. The dead man had been murdered and had been shot from outside the carriage by a gunman who had walked along the footboard. Police had already discounted this notion but had never attempted to replicate it. The younger men of the jury did succeed in showing that it was feasible to do exactly that, pull down the carriage window, fire the fatal shot and then drop the gun whilst trying to clamber back into the carriage behind.

Back in the courtroom it appeared as if a possible resolution had been found. The shot had been fired somewhere between Luton and the next station at Bedford. The killer had success-fully evaded capture, possibly leaving the train as it stood in Bedford station and had left the murder weapon behind. A reasonably sound theory until it was pointed out that on a moving train the kind of murder they were trying hard to prove was impossible to carry out. Anyone, argued the railway management, that attempted such a manoeuvre would have been knocked off the carriage side by any tree, tunnel or platform the train passed, add to this the fact that the gun had to have been fired twice to create the misfire and it was simply not possible. As if to pour more scorn on the idea three independent railway workers then told the court that they had examined the train carriage by carriage and from both sides of the track as it stood in the station at Bedford at twenty-two minutes past one on the morning of the killing. It was their job to grease the wheels and in order to do that they had been forced to clamber about beneath carriage No. 643 and, according to their testimony, they categorically denied that any gun could have lain on the running board and not have been seen by them.

As the inquest drew to a close the coroner examined final evidence as to the state of James Gray Lowe's business in an attempt to discover if any reason existed to commit suicide. As a businessman there was little doubt he had accumulated debts but no evidence existed to show that his company was in any sort of difficulty or that his creditors were demanding more. On the contrary it appeared he had been paying bills on time. The only suspicious circumstance police had uncovered was that he had taken out a number of life insurance policies but these, with a single exception, had been in existence for a number of years. This exception was the most recent which had been taken out in March of 1886, some six months earlier, for a sum of £8,000, but he had signed a clause precluding payment if he committed suicide within thirteen months of the start date.

Market Place Leicester c.1900. Author's collection

Market Place, Leicester

Turning to the jury at the close of the day the coroner asked the jurors to consider all the evidence not forgetting the broken umbrella. This item that had not been considered relevant by anyone who had presented a theory that day. Was it, he asked, relevant to the death? Had there been a fight of sorts inside the carriage prior to the shot being fired or had he committed suicide?

The jury returned a verdict that 'the deceased died by a revolver shot, but by whom it was fired there was not sufficient evidence to show'.

CHAPTER 6

The Death of a Policeman
The Murder of Constable Barratt
1886

Curtains twitched all along the street . . .

wenty-seven-year-old James Banton had lived a life on the edge of the law, nothing too serious, more a nuisance than a criminal. He was a man, it seemed, who always appeared to walk along that narrow line that separates the honest from the dishonest. No doubt he enjoyed the reputation he had gained amongst local police, revelling in his own notoriety when occasion demanded, but Banton was never considered a serious threat to the lives or livelihoods of those living around him. In the small village of Breedon-on-the-Hill where he lived he was well known to local beat

bobby, Thomas Barratt, where he was just one of a small number of trouble makers that occupied his patch from time to time. Barratt was not afraid of putting him in his place if circumstances required it. But Banton had always resented the policeman's intrusion into his life and made no attempt to hide his hatred of the man.

The church at Breedon-on-the-Hill. Author's collection

In February 1886 Banton had been caught with nets, a familiar tool for a poacher. Just how Constable Barratt had managed to catch him in possession is not recorded but most likely he had stumbled upon him in the act of setting them to catch rabbits. Either way the policeman took the nets away and with them went any possibility of a little black market trade. Banton never forgave him. Over the next six months the two men clashed whenever they met and, living in a small village, those meetings were frequent. Things came to a head on 15 August after a night spent in the *Lime Kiln Inn*.

Somewhat the worse for drink Banton accosted the policeman around nine o'clock in the evening along the road between the pub he had just left and the *Hollybush Inn* where he intended to go, some 300 yards away. Without any consideration for those that lived along the street he began shouting out the moment he saw the policeman's uniform. All too well aware that it belonged to Thomas Barratt he ran at him demanding at the top of his voice that he give back the nets that had been confiscated. Curtains twitched all along the street as neighbours heard the commotion and, at about that point, Joseph Gadsby, who had shared the bar with Banton at the

The Lime Kiln, *Breedon-on-the-Hill.* The author

Main Street looking toward where the Hollybush *stood.* The author

Limekiln Inn, joined him. Between the two of them they loudly harangued the policeman but Barratt was a very robust and powerful man, easily a match for the two drunks he believed were incapable of doing him any harm. Unconcerned by their implied threats he brushed them aside and after telling them to go home continued his beat. The two were lucky; Barratt could have arrested them at that point and quite possibly considered doing so. Probably the only reason he did not was a fear that a drunken rant may well have escalated into something more serious and more difficult for a lone policeman to handle. With hindsight it was a bad decision.

Gadsby, no doubt satisfied he had supported his friend sufficiently well, left Banton in the street and walked on to the *Hollybush Inn.* He and the landlord, Ben Hart, discussed the rights and wrongs of the argument with the policeman over a pint of beer. Meanwhile, Banton, seething at what he saw as Barratt's intransigence, continued to shout abuse at the constable's back, incensed at his own impotence when it came to avenging what he believed to be a serious injustice. As the policeman continued to ignore him and eventually turned off the street and onto the section of his beat that took him alongside the village stream Banton suddenly snapped. Finding a heavy stick in the gutter of the roadway he picked it up, felt its weight in the palm of his hand, and in a moment of pure madness charged after the policeman and struck him a single blow to the back of the head. Poleaxed, Barratt fell to the ground and in a frenzy of anger Banton then continued to rain blows at his head until he was dead. Mollified, he threw the stick away and, as if relieved of a burden that had been haunting him, ran back into the street singing at the top of his voice and made his way to join Gadsby.

But there was to be no drink to help his celebration. Ben Hart refused to allow him in the pub and locked the door against him, telling him that he was too drunk to be served. Angry at the refusal and full of righteous indignation, Banton then made the most catastrophic mistake of his life. He told the landlord from the other side of the door that he had just killed Thomas Barratt and dumped his body in the brook.

There was to be no hiding place from that moment on. Though Ben Hart did not believe him it took no time at all to find him and arrest him once the body had been found. According to the examining doctor, Barratt had been beaten almost beyond recognition, so extensive were his facial injuries. It was perfectly clear to the investigating officers that there had been no fight and that Banton had never allowed the policeman the opportunity of defending himself.

At his trial on 10 November, before Mr Justice Grantham, he pleaded not guilty, a formality that afforded him no hiding place in the courtroom though his defence team did attempt to show that death had been caused by a fall. The stream in which Barratt's body had been discovered lay some five and a half feet beneath a steep bank. It was the only defence available and it failed miserably. Too many witnesses took the stand through-out the day to testify to the fact that they had heard much of the argument that had taken place beneath their bedroom windows and others told the court of the antipathy felt by Banton toward the policeman. As to be expected the villagers were all too well aware of what had taken place between the two men over the months leading up to the murder.

In his summing up the judge told the jury that they had only one consideration to make:

> *Murder as defined by the law, was where a person of sound memory and discretion unlawfully kills another reasonable being with malice aforethought, either expressed or in the mind. They had first to find that the person accused of murder was of sound mind and discretion. It was not suggested that the prisoner was not that. Or that he was not liable for his actions, not withstanding that he was no doubt in a stupid and beery state, in which probably he had brought on himself by his drinking habits . . . As to the person killed, there was no doubt about the state of his health, or that he was a respectable and useful member of society. Further, there was no doubt that Banton did unlawfully kill him . . . And there was nothing shown that would relieve him of liability for this act. That being so, the question the jury had to consider was whether what he did was done in such a way as to show there*

Brook behind the **Limekiln Inn** *showing the steep bank.* The author

was malice in the eyes of the law ... It has been suggested by the defence that Barratt met with his death from a fall ... The back of the head was in such a position according to the doctor as to be above the part that would come into contact with a hard substance through a fall.

And so it went on. But the jury agreed that it could not have been accidental and that too much evidence, circumstantial as it was, pointed in Banton's direction. It took them an hour of deliberation to return a verdict of guilty.

Old village lock-up, Breedon-on-the-Hill. Author's collection

Chapter 7

The Fairfax Street Tragedy
The Murder of Ann Bloxham
1886

... she knelt momentarily before
Bloxham stepped forward ...

Sixty-two-year-old Thomas Bloxham had lived a chequered past by the time he arrived at Court B, Fairfax Street, Leicester, with his wife and eleven children, in July 1886. By trade a frame-work-knitter, he had spent much of his early life in pursuit of other pastimes, many of which had been against the law. But the occupation that had gained him both notoriety and prestige amongst many that knew him had been as a poacher. Known as *Rat* amongst the poaching gangs that roamed across Leicestershire's countryside, he

Granby Street, Leicester c.1910. Author's collection

had taken part in a number of the county's more publicised poaching escapades throughout the 1870s. So famous a reputation did he have by this time that whenever a serious poaching affray hit the headlines he was inevitably bound up in the story even if he had taken no part in it. The first time he was ever brought before a magistrate was October 1873 after being arrested for carrying a shotgun, a crime for which he was fined thirty shillings (£1.50). This was followed in December of the same year when he was caught a second time for exactly the same thing and fined £3. Five months later he led a poaching gang onto land at Foxton in the early hours of the morning only to be caught by gamekeepers who had been tipped off. This resulted in a pitched battle and one of the keepers, James Ward, was badly injured. That put Bloxham in prison for two months, with hard labour. He followed that in 1876 by being sentenced to twelve months after being arrested in Groby for a similar crime. Then, reputation greatly enhanced, he managed to evade the law for two years, only to be caught once more after a fierce and desperate fight with gamekeepers at Kilby. After another short spell in prison he returned to his earlier stamping ground around Foxton where he carried out a number of successful poaching escapades before once again gamekeepers laid a trap for him and hauled him off to the magistrates' court where he was returned to prison. On this occasion though the court ordered he find sureties for his good behaviour for a period of twelve months after his release or else be returned to his cell for a significant spell of imprisonment. By now in his late fifties it was enough of a threat to force him to rethink his life and he returned to his former occupation as a frame-work-knitter.

There was also something else going on in his life that helped dictate the change. Whilst developing this infamous reputation he had also begun to live with a woman named Ann Bowley or Ann Page dependent upon which name she chose to use. Bowley was her maiden name but Ann had been married and it is believed that at the time she began her involvement with Bloxham that marriage was still on the statute books. Whether or not Bloxham was aware of this is unclear. Either way, the two entered into marriage at some point in the early 1870s and over the next sixteen years, pregnancy became a constant companion for Ann. It also led to a series of violent arguments within the home and on more than one occasion, throughout their married life, she had been forced to seek police protection. These fights and the police involvement they brought inevitably put Bloxham back in prison for short spells. So by the time the couple made the house move to Fairfax Street it is fair to say the relationship was somewhat strained.

Within four months of their arrival at their new home Bloxham was accusing his wife of being unfaithful. After following her one afternoon he saw her meet with a man he knew by the nickname of Jack Country, a man he was familiar with and who often drank in the same public houses that Bloxham was in the habit of visiting. She denied it and told him that the meeting had been accidental and that he was to read nothing into it. But it was all a little too late for Bloxham. He had convinced himself weeks earlier that she was involved in an affair and her denial did nothing to change his view. Determined to confront John Burdett, alias Jack Country, he left a bruised and battered Ann at home and went off in search of revenge. The two men met at William Spence's beer-house on Havelock Street. Burdett, a younger man, was not easily

Havelock Street, Leicester as it looks today. The author

Gallowtree Gate, Leicester c.1920. Author's collection

cowed into submission and Bloxham, perhaps realising that he was likeliest of the two to suffer in a fight, backed off. Desperate to exact justice, as he saw it, he walked to Clarke's gunsmith shop on Gallowtree Gate and bought himself a pistol and a pennyworth of large shot. For Ann Bloxham there was going to be no place to hide.

On the following day, 26 November 1886, at seven o'clock in the evening, she walked in through the back door of the house after visiting a neighbour and was instantly shot in the chest. There was no conversation between the two. Bloxham, who had patiently waited for her return, simply stepped out in front of her and fired the pistol once. The bullet entered her left lung. Dropping to her knees she knelt momentarily before Bloxham stepped forward, pushed her onto her back, straddled her and cut her throat with a knife.

The Sir Robert Peel, *one of the pubs frequented by Bloxham.* The author

Eliza Green, the woman Ann had been visiting that afternoon, lived only fifteen yards away. As the sound of the gunshot
died away she saw one of the Bloxham's children, fourteen-
year-old daughter Kate, run screaming from the house. Raising
the alarm amongst her neighbours, Eliza instinctively made a
dash for the house and as she pushed her way in through the
door saw the full horror of what had taken place only seconds
earlier. According to her later statement Bloxham was still sat
astride his wife who lay on the floor, and was in the process of
slashing at her throat. He paused only to stare back at her as she
shouted at him to stop. For Ann of course it was all too late.
The bullet wound would certainly have killed in time but the
knife had done its job by the time Eliza Green had arrived on
the scene.

When the local constable, Robert Neal, walked into the
house minutes later Bloxham was standing with his back to the
fireplace, holding the gun in his right hand. Easily disarmed,
he made no attempt to resist arrest and freely admitted that he
had been responsible for the murder of his wife, telling the
young policeman in graphic detail how he had fired the fatal
shot and then cut her throat. Landlord William Spence, who

knew Bloxham well and had arrived at the house minutes earlier, then shouted out that he had given up the gun but not the razor and there was a moment's panic as everyone stood back. But Bloxham was in no frame of mind by this time to threaten anyone else. Denying he had used a razor he turned to face the fireplace. 'It's in there!' he shouted angrily. Constable Neal followed his gaze and saw the bright edge of a blade amongst the coals.

At his trial, which opened to a packed courtroom on 25 January 1887 before Mr Justice Field, Thomas Bloxham was forced to conduct his own defence. Lack of money prevented him hiring a QC to perform this function and obviously placed him at a distinct disadvantage before the case had even begun. Even so, it had not prevented him building a defence that he believed would keep him away from the scaffold. After pleading not guilty and listening to testimony from an array of witnesses, most of whom had been his neighbours, and almost all of whom he failed to cross examine with any effectiveness, he took the stand himself.

A hush fell across the courtroom as those watching realised that the evidence that had been presented thus far was damning in the extreme and recognising that he would have to offer up something extraordinary if he were to escape the noose. He did

Gallowtree Gate, Leicester today. The author

not disappoint. After some preamble about his past and what he still believed had been his wife's infidelities he told the court he could not have murdered her because she had committed suicide. It was a stunning revelation, particularly in light of the fact that he had apparently been seen in the act of committing murder, which of course he denied. When Eliza Green had entered his kitchen, he told the jurors, it had been to see him attempting to retrieve the knife she had used in order that he could then use it on himself, it had not been to witness a murder. The two, he insisted, had made a pact to end their lives together. The pistol had been intended as the best means of suicide because it ought to have been quick and easy. He admitted it had been he that loaded the weapon, but insisted he had never fired it. Ann, he told the hushed court, had snatched it from the kitchen table where he had carefully placed it between the two of them. Unfortunately, as she raised it toward her head it had fired accidentally, the bullet hitting her in her chest, which had not killed her instantly. Determined to end her life she had then snatched up a knife from a nearby shelf and cut her own throat. As for himself, after watching this carnage he claimed to have lost his nerve and as a result had become confused and unable to think clearly. Admitting to murder had been the result of all this confusion and had not been a true account of exactly what had happened on 26 November.

The jury rejected it without even retiring to consider their verdict. There was no public support for a petition demanding a reprieve and on Valentine's Day, Monday 14 February 1887, as the prison bell tolled eight o'clock on a cold morning, a crowd of over two thousand stood in silence as the black flag was raised to mark his execution.

CHAPTER 8

The Jealous Husband
The Murder of Isabella Newell
1894

... he calmly dropped the hammer to the floor.

ohn Newell had an exemplary military record with the Royal Marines where he served a number of years in Egypt. This in turn had gained him the rank of sergeant and an even greater number of years in the garrison at Plymouth. Here it was at some point during the mid 1870s that he met a West Country girl, Isabella, and fell madly in love. The two eventually married towards the end of that decade and over the next sixteen years or so, successfully raised a family of three girls and two boys. Then, as age caught up with him and military service became more arduous than it had once been, he accepted the post of recruiting sergeant, a position he held until 1891 when he made the decision to leave the service and accept a pension. At the grand old age of forty he suddenly found himself a pensioner, but a pensioner with a little money. The service had been kind to him over the years and he and Isabella had managed to tuck away a reasonably sized nest egg. With the children still young, his eldest daughter Blanche only fourteen at that time, the couple decided to make a break from all things military and buy a grocer's shop. They both knew that a business would provide them with adequate income for the remainder of their lives, particularly when that income was added to the soldier's pension he had begun to receive. The shop premises they chose was at 53 Woodgate, Loughborough. Exactly why they made the decision to move so far north is not known but it

High Street, Loughborough, c.1928. Author's collection

certainly proved successful. The shop thrived from the minute they took the controls and the combination income began to create a comfortable lifestyle for the whole family. When they supplemented that by the addition of rent from two lodgers, Herbert Hoares, 'Lemmy' to those that knew him well, and Edith Tyers, a young woman that had become a close friend of daughter Blanche, things were certainly on the up. But it was at that point, with life seemingly on an ever-upward trend, that cracks began to appear in the relationship.

Not much is known about Hoares and he did not stay around the house for very long, but without doubt it was certainly he that caused these cracks. Within two years of his being introduced into the family, and long after he had left it, an otherwise solid, reliable relationship had fragmented into one of serious mistrust. Newell, apparently without any evidence, began to suspect that Hoares and Isabella were conducting an affair within weeks of their first meeting. It cast a dark cloud over an otherwise happy marriage and despite his wife's continued denial of any kind of impropriety he found himself unable to accept that his fears were unfounded. Consumed by a sudden and violent jealousy he took to the bottle, and for the next two years life behind the grocer's counter became increasingly fraught.

By the summer of 1894 the couple were on a disastrous collision course. In May of the same year Isabella had been forced to call in police after her husband had arrived back at the shop in a drunken rage. Charged with violent conduct, he had been bound over to keep the peace for three months. Eight weeks after his court appearance he had burst into the shop after a night drinking whisky and armed with a carving knife, had chased her around the shop's counter. Only the intervention of neighbours and his daughter Blanche had disarmed him, and in turn saved him from prison. But the anger never went away.

John and Isabella Newell. Author's collection

On the night of 20 August the arguments began again. When Blanche, by now sixteen years old, and Edith Tyers, the lodger, arrived back at the house after a day at work, Newell was standing in the closed shop staring out of the window. Isabella was in the kitchen preparing the evening meal and both were continuing a row that had been simmering all day, shouting at each other from their respective rooms. It went on until about half past ten at night, at which time, tired of the constant bickering, all the children and the lodger had retired to their respective bedrooms. Isabella, probably by now desperate to end the constant arguing, confronted Newell as the house fell silent and told him in no uncertain words that she had had enough. Citing his constant jealous rage as the catalyst that had caused her to rethink her future, she told him that she would be removing her name from above the shop door and leaving in the morning. Almost as a rider to this she then added that when she left the children would be leaving with her. It was a statement designed to create the greatest impact on the man she had grown to hate and it did exactly that, but not as she had intended.

When Isabella went to her bed that night it was not the bed she normally shared with her husband. Not surprisingly, she had no wish to be in the same room as the man she had threatened

Town Hall and Market Place, Loughborough, c.1928. Author's collection

to leave and so decided to sleep with her daughter Lucy and younger son, eight-year-old William. The sleeping arrangements at Woodgate were, as would be expected with a large family, always somewhat cramped. The house had three bedrooms, two at the front and one at the back. Isabella chose the room directly above the shop; Newell slept next door with their youngest child, three-year-old Stephen, and elder daughter Blanche shared with her ten-year-old sister Clara and the lodger Edith at the back of the house. It would have been impossible for Newell to exact any sort of revenge upon his wife during that night without attracting attention from one of the bedrooms centred on the short landing. So he waited and as he passed a sleepless night, plotted revenge.

At around a quarter past six next morning Blanche and Edith, the only two that had to leave the house to go to work, were up and about. With the factory only yards from the shop, like many that had to make an early start, they always stole an extra minute in bed before rising and making tea. That morning was no exception. Before leaving, Blanche took a cup of tea up to her mother as she often did and found her sitting beside the bedroom window watching the early risers fill the street below. The two exchanged a few words before Blanche ran back downstairs and she and Edith went off to work. Almost as the front door closed Newell strode out of the adjoining bedroom, walked in on Isabella as she drank her tea and struck her five times on the head with a coal pick he had taken from the coal house in the yard the night before. As he struck the first blow he asked calmly; 'Now what did you say you would do to me last night?' As she quickly lost consciousness, he calmly dropped the pick to the floor. His son, William, had witnessed the whole scene. Frightened out of their wits, all the children then ran from the house in their nightclothes and sought sanctuary with a neighbour whilst Newell, taking a fresh bottle of whisky from a sideboard, walked out into the street.

Police Constable Lewis Weston passed him some thirty yards from the house and exchanged a 'Good morning' before being made aware of just what had occurred minutes earlier. He then arrested him shortly afterwards in the garden of a local priest, Reverend Penny. Newell offered up no resistance but did admit his guilt:

> *Here I am; I have killed the ******* all through that Lemmy Hoares . . . I have had enough of it for the last eighteen months. I will go to the gallows with a good heart if she is dead.*

By the time the young policeman had walked his prisoner to Loughborough police station Isabella Newell was dead.

At one-thirty on the afternoon of 20 November Mr Justice Cave took his seat before a packed courtroom. Forty-two-year-old John William Newell, dressed smartly in a grey suit, took his place in the dock and in a calm voice pleaded, 'Not guilty'. During the intervening three months his defence team had been trying hard to piece together a defence strategy that would keep him from the gallows. Having freely admitted his guilt and

Leicester Prison. The author

having committed the murder before his own son, they all knew that some sort of plea in mitigation had to be found. That came only after rigorous investigations had been carried out into the background of Newell's life and family history. Insanity, as the defence team knew well enough, was the only guarantee against execution if it could be proved. When the trial opened they had built their case around the fact that in Newell's family no less than seven blood relations had gone mad. His aunt, Mary Tilbury, was in the Hanwell mental asylum; Jane Nash, a second cousin, was an inmate of the Stone asylum, as had been Emma Payne, another second cousin and great uncle William Hussey, both of whom had actually died there. Other relatives: Annie James, Thomas James and John Hussey, all cousins of one sort or another had all apparently died as a result of madness having all spent some time in their lives locked away. So, on the face of it, sufficient evidence existed to show there had to be a possibility that all this tendency toward madness was hereditary. According to the defence team, Newell had been suffering a form of insanity at the time of the attack and his own antecedents, according to what they had uncovered, proved beyond doubt that this manic tendency had always existed in his own family bloodline. Unfortunately for them, proving that madness had existed over the years was one thing, proving it had been inherited and had manifested itself in the murder of Isabella was another.

After hearing witness evidence from the children and the key testimony from young William Newell, the son who had watched the whole events of the morning of 21 August unfold, prosecution counsel Mr Leedham called two doctors to the stand. The first was Leicester's prison surgeon, Dr Moore. He told the court that having had Newell under observation almost since his arrest there had never been any signs of insanity and that in his opinion the man had suffered no mental breakdown, an opinion then corroborated by a Dr Finch, this second piece of testimony being the key piece of medical evidence. Of the two men, Finch's testimony, as Medical Officer to the Leicester Lunatic Asylum, carried the greater weight and he therefore was judged to have irrefutable knowledge of mental illness and in particular insanity. The defence counsel, despite building their case around Newell's mental decline, was unable to produce any medical evidence to refute the psychiatrist's findings. This was a serious and extremely damaging blow and one from which they never recovered. In his summing up to the jurors, which took no longer than fifteen minutes, Mr Justice Cave told them that the notion that a man was sane all his life, insane at the time of the crime, then sane again, was not acceptable. They heeded the advice and after retiring for ten minutes returned a verdict of guilty. Newell was duly sentenced to death.

A petition for clemency was immediately raised and sub-mitted to the Home Secretary. Meanwhile, Newell settled down to a prison regime. Being a soldier for much of his life meant that this regime was not difficult for him to handle. Discipline had been at the heart of his daily life for so many years that to take orders and obey them presented little hardship, and he fitted quickly into the prison routine. A model prisoner, he caused no concern to the prison authorities and when news of the Home Secretary's decision not to grant clemency was delivered to him on the eve of his execution, he accepted it without too much of an emotional reaction.

In a conversation before his execution, with his good friend, Reverend Sydney Mees, he made a full and frank confession.

He admitted that he had suffered no breakdown and that he had murdered his wife after suffering a sleepless night brought on by what he believed to be a serious threat to his relationship with his wife and his family's security. When she had told him that she would take her name down from the shop door and leave with the children, he had believed her. So much so that he was determined to stop her and that killing her was the only way he could think this could be achieved. Though he added, on the morning he had walked into the bedroom to kill her he had expected the door to be closed against him. It was not and that, apparently, cost her her life.

At eight o'clock on the morning of 10 December James Billington, the state executioner, pulled the lever that sent him to his death. Outside, 5,000 people gathered on a cold winter morning and watched the raising of the black flag signifying that sentence had been carried out.

John Newell as he looked at his trial.
Author's collection

THE

LOUGHBOROUGH MURDER.

EXECUTION OF NEWELL

THIS MORNING,

STARTLING CONFESSION BY THE CRIMINAL.

HIS STORY OF THE CRIME.

THE CONVICT'S CAREER.

CHAPTER 9

Battle's Sixpenny Killer
The Suspicious Death of
John Jesson
1900

... before the clock struck ten he was dead.

ohn and Elizabeth Mary Jesson were married on Whit Monday 1899. Like thousands of marriages before and since, it was a perfect love match, or so it seemed. The happy couple went to live on a farm at Ratcliffe-on-the-Wreake and John, a skilled carpenter, took on the role of a farm labourer. For six months all was well in the Jesson household but by the dawn of 1900 the marriage was in difficulties. Exactly what those difficulties were is not known but certainly the couple had a difference of opinion over children. John was keen that they start a family as soon as was possible, Elizabeth less so. She had begun to resort to a variety of methods to prevent pregnancy including taking saltpetre as a method of birth control. Argument followed argument and by March of the New Year John had upped and left. Deciding that neither farming nor marriage was for him he left the farm and took up a carpentry job at Leicester. Elizabeth, without sufficient income, was forced to abandon the house on the farm and return to her parents' farmhouse, Bleak House, Illston-on-the-Hill. But she determined that their marriage was not over and began a series of letters to her estranged husband pleading for him to return. The first, written on 27 March, is a good indicator as to how strong her feelings were for John and shows the depths of her despair:

Radcliffe-on-the-Wreake today. The author

My own dear husband. It is such a trouble to be parted from you. We were joined together on the 22 May and parted on the 22 March. Oh! That my grief were thoroughly weighed my calamity laid in the balance together for now it would be heavier than the sands of the sea. Therefore, my words are swallowed up. Curse the night in which I was conceived; let darkness come upon me. If I cannot live with you, I will not live without you, as my life is misery to me. If I had not gone away from the lodge I should have been in my grave by this. Now, I wish I was. You must come, or I shall go out of my mind. I shall go to Leicester on Saturday, and you must come down to the George to see me. . . . I remain your true and loving wife.

Elizabeth

Illston-on-the-Hill today. The author

John probably abhorred the sentiment for he certainly ignored the appointment at the *George*. It seems likely that he had no intentions of accepting any attempts at reconciliation, either by his wife or his friends. He had embarked upon a new and different road to the one he had stepped off some weeks earlier and had no wish to return to it. He talked openly amongst friends about Elizabeth, his feelings for her, which appeared to be less than amatory and how he resented her family. All this, of course, found its way back to Elizabeth and she in turn chastised him through her letters. Whether this had any real effect upon John is uncertain but at some point in late April he made the first of what would be three returns to his in-laws' house at Illston-on-the-Hill. None of these so-called weekend visits appear to have been intended to resolve their differences but more to placate Elizabeth, perhaps an attempt at appeasement rather than reconciliation. At first she was happy for the visits to take place but less than enamoured after the second one when she began to realise that they were not actually achieving her intention, which was to win back her husband. She wrote to him to tell him that things had changed:

Dear John,
I have made up my mind not to trouble you about anything any more. I am going to take things easy, live long and die happy . . .

*You have quite offended my father and mother by treating me as
you have done. Time was that every minute you had to spare you
was over here after me, and now will not walk a mile to speak to
me . . .*

This prompted a double response from John. Possibly stung by
her apparent sudden lack of interest in himself or their marriage,
he wrote two letters, one to Elizabeth and one to her mother,
which was later destroyed. In the letter to his wife, obviously
having had time to think, he dragged up the causes of their
split, leastways as he saw them, and indicated that the prime
cause had been her lack of interest when it came to family,
accusing her once more of having stooped to various birth
control methods behind his back including the use of strychnine. In her written response she refuted the allegation and
wrote that she had never used poison as a method to prevent
pregnancy. This mention of poison was to later play a far more
serious rôle in both their lives.

At the beginning of May, Elizabeth, probably in a last ditch
attempt at reconciliation, wrote inviting John to visit her at
her parents' home for a third time. John agreed. There then
followed a series of letters about her feelings and how she still
sought a return to their marriage. Whether John responded in
kind is not known but would appear unlikely. On 17 May, with
the date of John's visit set for 26 May, she wrote a last letter
couched in the usual affectionate terms with a more purposeful
request at the end of it:

*. . . Now I have a new trouble come, there is a mouse in my
bedroom. Get me some Battle's Vermin Killer, 6d a packet, from
Berridge's. I will pay you for it. We shall have mice all over the
house after a bit. Nobody seems to care about it and we have no
cat. I should not have cared if they would keep out of my bedroom.
Please get Battle's as the other is no good. You will have to sign
your name for it, but I don't care about that if I can get rid of the
mouse.*

John apparently bought the vermin killer, which came in a small
packet, and took it with him to his in-laws' farmhouse. Exactly

what time he arrived at the house is not known but the family all sat down together to eat supper at eight o'clock; he was made welcome, as he knew he would be, and had arranged to stay the night with Elizabeth, something that had come to be expected each time he visited. At around half-past nine that same night the household, as was common on a farm, retired to bed. Elizabeth left John in the kitchen whilst she went up to the bedroom and as she undressed for bed heard him draw the latch on the back door and walk out into the yard. Some quarter of an hour later she heard him return and after locking up behind him he went straight upstairs to her room. The two talked as he undressed and after being in bed about a quarter of an hour he began to complain of feeling unwell. Elizabeth went into her parents' bedroom and fetched her mother. But there was nothing that could be done for John and before the clock struck ten he was dead.

Dr Leonard William Oliver, practising at Billesdon, was sent for and he arrived at eleven o'clock that night. When he began his examination John Jesson lay on his back on the bed with his arms folded across his chest, his hands clenched and his thumbs turned in. His head was drawn back, and his eyes partly closed. The lips were blue, the body cool and he agreed that time of death had been approximately one hour earlier. After a

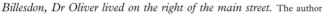

Billesdon, Dr Oliver lived on the right of the main street. The author

cursory examination he satisfied himself that there had been no external injuries that could have caused the death but remained extremely suspicious about just how that death had been brought about. He knew all too well that strychnine acts rapidly on the central nervous system, not only does it cause violent convulsions, which quickly expend the body's muscular energy, it also results in an almost immediate onset of rigor mortis. As far as Dr Oliver was concerned what he saw before him exhibited all the classic signs of strychnine poisoning and so, therefore, he alerted the police. They, in turn, had a full post-mortem carried out and the internal organs examined by Home Office scientific analyst, Dr Thomas Stevenson. As expected, he found poison in every organ he examined. According to his police report he also found a quantity of wheat or barley flour, a dark pigment, which was Prussian blue and, of course, 2 grains of strychnine. This was the exact make-up of *Battle's Vermin Killer.* According to the analyst the *Battle* brand was actually a powder that contained all these ingredients, which were meant to make it palatable to rats and mice. It could also be dissolved in water or whisky and one of the other liquids found in John Jesson's stomach, apart from the supper he had eaten, was the remains of a glass of Scotch. Elizabeth Jesson was immediately arrested and charged with murder.

On 3 August, after being assisted into the courtroom, she stood briefly in the dock at the small East Norton court-house having already been pronounced guilty by the coroner's inquest, and pleaded her innocence. Clearly ill as the case began, she was allowed to sit throughout the whole proceedings and, clutching a white handkerchief to her face, hardly ever lifted her head up to view the courtroom. Fortunately for her she was ably defended by a Mr J T Hincks, who, it would appear, never doubted her innocence.

The prosecution case was simple enough. They claimed that after the marriage break-up and the failure of her letter campaign to win back her husband, she resorted to murder. The motive, they argued, was simple revenge. She had decided that if he were to stay away from the marital home, which would at some point have precipitated a divorce, then she would stop him the only way possible, and that way, they insisted, was

The old police station at East Norton. The author

murder. Elizabeth Jesson, they told the court, had devised a plan to kill her husband by using poison. The easiest method, and the most effective, was to use strychnine. A poison, they claimed, that she knew would be readily available to her if she could obtain it through a chemist claiming it was necessary to eradicate vermin. The plan was a devious one because she was also all too well aware that to obtain poison or any merchandise using it as part of a product's make-up, she would have to sign the poison register. So, she wrote a letter asking her husband to do it for her. This, claimed the prosecution, kept her hands clean, so to speak: no record would ever exist that could prove she had purchased the substance that killed her own husband. It was certainly a sensible argument and was borne out by a number of the known facts. To support the assertion all her letters were read out in open court, doctors were brought to the stand to confirm the post-mortem findings and police testified that no poisonous substances had been owned by Jesson before he arrived at the farmhouse. In other words, he had not been harbouring a substance that he could use upon himself to commit suicide.

But the discerning Mr Hincks, apart from not believing any of it, systematically destroyed the whole prosecution case with an astute piece of cross-examination. He knew that for Elizabeth Jesson to be found guilty then the way in which the poison was administered had to be proven. The prosecution had appeared to prove beyond doubt during the questioning of the Home Office analyst that it had been administered via a glass of whisky. But under close cross examination Dr Stevenson told the court that whilst strychnine would not alter the smell of Scotch it would alter its taste. When immersed in whisky, he told the magistrates, it gave an extremely bitter taste, so bitter in fact that anyone attempting to drink it would have had great difficulty in swallowing it.

Hincks knew at that point that he had killed off the idea of Scotch as a vehicle for murder. With this success behind him he then went on to outline to the court that if that were the case then Jesson could not have been poisoned by his wife. He itemised the evening's events at the farm and made great show of the fact that John Jesson was both capable and well at nine-thirty on the night of his death, the time his wife went up to bed. Strychnine, he went on, took no longer than twenty minutes to take effect and death followed on no more than ten to twenty minutes later. Where, he asked the court, did Elizabeth Jesson have the time to administer the deadly dose? If his wife was in bed at 9.30 pm and he was well at that time and if he was still well when he walked into the bedroom how could she have poisoned him?

The seeds of doubt were well and truly sown. In his closing speech to the court Hincks argued that when John Jesson had walked out into the yard he had done so with a purpose. *Battle's Vermin Killer*, he told the magistrates, was bought in small packets, the strength of the poison is therefore deceiving and strychnine was certainly used by a number of people as a pick-

Illston-on-the-Hill church. The author

me-up. Jesson, he asserted, had used the packet for just such a purpose but had misjudged the dose because he had presumed that so small a packet could not contain a lethal level of poison when consumed by humans. When he had then complained of being unwell his wife, Elizabeth, had done what any other woman would have done, she gave him a glass of whisky to help ease his pain, which is why the pathologist found Scotch in Jesson's stomach.

What he never explained was that no empty packet of *Battle's Vermin Killer* was ever found, neither was the glass or cup from which Jesson drank and no chemist had been found showing Jesson's signature in their poison register, but the court accepted the argument. They agreed that there was insufficient evidence to show that Elizabeth Jesson had committed murder and she was released; the death, of course, has remained a mystery.

CHAPTER 10

A Poacher's Revenge
The Murder of Constable
Wilkinson
1903

Suddenly, out of the corner of his eye, he thought he saw a movement in the churchyard.

Twenty-four-year-old Thomas Preston had arrived back in his home village in 1902 after four years in the army. Sent to South Africa in 1899, where he had served Queen and country against the Boers, Preston had returned to take up his old occupation in the shoe industry and pick up the reins of his old life. What returned with him was a penchant for drink. He had grown accustomed to alcohol in the army and had no intentions of giving it up. Neither had his close friend, Thomas Porter, who shared the same interest. The two became regular drinkers at Sileby's public houses, which in turn brought them inevitably to the attention of local police on more than one occasion.

Like many villages around the country beat officers, policemen who lived close to the job, regularly policed Sileby's streets. Their job, as well as keeping close contact with the community, was to know not only the area, but also the people, businesses, petty thieves and drunks. Preston and Porter fell into this latter category. Drunk more than sober meant they were constantly monitored and frequently arrested on drunk and disorderly charges. This gave them a deserved reputation as trouble makers and when the two were caught after making the occasional foray into the woods to poach, this reputation was enhanced, particularly in policing circles.

William Wilkinson had served in Leicestershire's police force for ten years, much of this time being spent in Sileby. He and fellow officer PC Hall knew the men extremely well. They had both been responsible for arresting the two on more than one occasion and were often all too well aware of what was happening in the men's lives. Sileby in 1903 was a close community of about 3,000 people and with police on the ground, unlike today; it was all part of the job to know what was happening in the village. Hall and Wilkinson were very adept at doing exactly that, much to the chagrin of the two heavy drinkers who began to believe that there was a conspiracy to harass them wherever they went. The sense of injustice felt by both finally bubbled to the surface in February of the same year after a close friend was arrested for holding a gun without a licence.

Believing that PC Wilkinson, the arresting officer, had been too officious in forcing the case to court and that his real intention had really been to hit at them because of their poaching activities, there was an argument on the court steps. Porter, incensed by what he saw as persecution, pushed the young policeman against a wall and told him in no uncertain terms that he was going to shoot him. The threat, witnessed by a number of people, was thought at the time to be nothing but a piece of bravado from an angry man. Certainly the policeman made nothing of it and appeared to simply shrug it off as part of the job. It was a mistake for which he would pay a heavy price. Porter had meant every word he had said and from the moment he left the court steps he began to plan the murder that would rock Leicester for months to come.

Both Porter and Preston, as would perhaps have been expected, knew the normal police routines. They were all too well aware that both PC Wilkinson and PC Hall worked together and that whenever that entailed a night shift the two policemen had a habit of meeting at Sileby's parish church. On the night of 25 February, with this in mind, Porter met with Thomas Preston in the *Sir John Moore* to plan the revenge they had threatened so openly. At around half-past nine the two men, in company with a third man, Fred Dexter, who was not party to the plot, moved on to the *Railway Inn*. At a little after

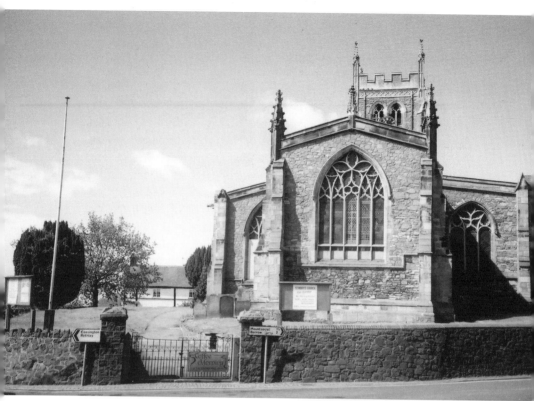

Sileby church. The author

ten o'clock and after purchasing three bottles of stout, the three men then walked the short distance to Sileby church. Once there they all three sat by the wall and drank the beer. There followed a general discussion, which Dexter later recalled as being to do with poaching and some fifteen minutes or so later Dexter was told to go home. Reluctant and believing that the two were about to go fetch Porter's gun and then shoot rabbits, Dexter at first refused. All three by this time were the worse for wear after several pints of beer, but their insistence that he not get himself involved because he had no police record, finally convinced him. Once their drinking partner had left they walked the short distance to Porter's house on Swan Street, retrieved the shotgun then returned to the church and hid behind a tombstone.

The Railway Inn, *Sileby.* The author

Constable Wilkinson, after doing a round of the village pubs, never varied from his routine. Just as Porter and Preston knew he would, he made his slow way to the church gates at Sileby church, the rendezvous point where he and Constable Hall had arranged to meet, as they always did, at around 11 pm. As he arrived at the gates, some fifteen minutes earlier than he had planned, Wilkinson was met by local butcher, Herbert Middleton returning home after a late night in his

The gravestones behind which Preston and Porter hid. The author

shop preparing meat for the following day. Happy enough to pass the time of day with a familiar face and knowing that he had time to spare, the two stood chatting by the gate waiting for Constable Hall to make an appearance. Wilkinson, who had a habit of not standing still for long, paced as he talked. Suddenly, out of the corner of his eye, he thought he saw a movement in the churchyard. Telling the butcher to stay where he was he then cast the light from his lamp across the surrounding gravestones and began to walk slowly toward the church. Some ten feet from the gate he was shot dead after being hit in the heart by shot from both barrels of a shotgun.

The dead policeman was carried into the *Plough Inn* where Dr Walter Garvin removed forty pieces of shot from his chest, six having entered his heart and all, according to the doctor, fired from close range. Within the hour police were swarming across the village. Short on leads and with little evidence found at the murder scene they made what amounted to a calculated guess that it had been a revenge killing. Superintendent Agar, brought from Loughborough, put together a list of names, those he believed could have had a hand in the murder and topping that list were the two poachers. Arriving at Preston's home in the early hours a quick search revealed that he had not slept in his bed that night. Alerted by neighbours that he had been seen earlier in the company of Porter, Agar then took the investigating team to Swan Street. Here they found the house in darkness but not about to be so easily put off, Agar had the front door broken down and as he pushed his way into an upstairs bedroom found himself staring down both barrels of a gun. Porter, who held the shotgun to his shoulder told the policeman to back off, encouraged by Preston standing a little way behind him, and forced the police to retreat. The siege of Swan Street had begun.

Wisely, Superintendent Agar made the sensible decision from the outset that there was to be no armed response and that the two were simply to be contained. Surrounding the house and closing off neighbouring streets, he was able to control the situation well enough and set up a regular dialogue with the two men. The longer this dialogue went on the more it became

Swan Street, Sileby. The author

evident to the policeman that he had cornered PC Wilkinson's killers. Porter, in particular, seemed unable to keep his mouth shut and left him in no doubt it had been an intentional murder and that the siege was well justified. All this went on throughout the night and, despite the superintendent's continued caution for the two to keep quiet and not continue to incriminate themselves. Finally, after several hours and probably as the two sobered up, police patience paid off. The gun was broken in half by Porter and thrown out of the window and Superintendent Agar made his arrest.

At the trial in Leicester on 29 June before Mr Justice Ridley and a packed courtroom the two stood in the dock and pleaded not guilty. It was a trial, not so much about their culpability, but about exactly who fired the fatal shot and had both conspired to commit the murder? The prosecution contention was that it certainly had been a conspiracy and that both men had decided to kill the young constable. In their opening speech to the jury they made it crystal clear that there was to be no absolution for either man. Both, they argued, had agreed to murder and therefore both were equally guilty.

The only serious challenge to that premise came from Preston on the second day of the trial. From the witness stand he contended that he had not been a party to the murder and that the gun had been collected from Porter's house only to poach. When Porter fired the fatal shot he claimed not to have been beside him behind the tombstone. According to Preston's testimony he had been frightened off when Wilkinson had cast his lamplight about the churchyard and had run away. In the dark he claimed that he had scaled the church wall to escape and had heard the shot go off behind him. Porter agreed with this version in his own statement made to police before the trial began, adding that the two of them had been so drunk on the night that they were not responsible for their actions. Unfortunately for both men whilst Preston was on the stand he was asked quite pointedly by the judge if being drunk meant that his general recall of events was poor. When he answered in the affirmative the judge asked him to explain, if that were the case, how it was that both of them appeared to have complete recall when it came to the shooting of Constable Wilkinson. He had no answer and there the defence floundered. It was totally destroyed after Superintendent Agar told the court that during the house siege, which had gone on until 7 am of the day following the killing, there seemed little doubt to him that they had intended not only Wilkinson's death but also that of Hall, according to the notations he had made as the men hurled abuse at his officers from the bedroom window at stages throughout the night. Both men admitted their guilt.

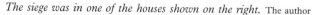

The siege was in one of the houses shown on the right. The author

In his summing up to the jury Mr Justice Ridley told them they must consider, in light of the evidence, whether or not both men had intended to commit a murder or had they intended to go poaching and the shot fired had been accidental, in which case they could return a verdict of manslaughter. But if they believed that revenge had been exacted that night then regardless of who fired the fatal shot they must return a guilty verdict against them both. There was no doubting the outcome and after a brief adjournment the jury returned with a guilty verdict.

Both men were executed together by William Billington at Leicester on Tuesday 21 July 1903. Both protested their innocence on the scaffold.

Newspaper drawing of the murder scene and those involved. Leicester Mercury

CHAPTER 11

The Mysterious Affair at Croft
The Murder of Annie Haines
1907

... he strangled her on the road and pushed her body in the ditch.

When Annie Elizabeth Haines met and fell in love with Archie Page she was fifteen years old and so was he. The two had known each other since school days and to their respective families the relationship was, perhaps understandably, initially seen as a simple schoolgirl crush. By the dawn of 1907, some two years later, with the relationship apparently ever strengthening, the view from the family had modified somewhat. Archie was accepted by Annie's family who had begun to realise, and more importantly accept, that the pair were serious about their feelings and the prospect of a future marriage was no longer regarded with a healthy scepticism. Annie had managed to convince everyone that knew her that this was one relationship she was not about to give up.

Born at Sutton-in-the-Elms, she had been brought up in the Baptist church and had been

THE VICTIM
(ANNIE ELIZABETH HAINES)

Annie Elizabeth Haines. Leicester Mercury

a regular Sunday school pupil so it seemed only reasonable she should want to stay around the church. When the family moved out to Croft toward the end of her schooldays she took work as a domestic servant to the Reverend Jenkins at Hinkley. The work was light, easily manageable and she enjoyed being around the vicarage. Rail links being plentiful at this time, unlike today, also meant that there were good train connections between home and work. If ever she needed to be nearer family she also had her aunt, Martha Gibbins, living in Attleborough who kept a spare room for her niece whenever needed. Archie, meanwhile, had taken work at the local colliery and the two met regularly at Croft or else he would travel to Attleborough if she were staying away.

But this cosy, easy love affair was about to change. Toward the end of September 1907 Annie saw a different side to Archie's character for the first time and what she saw frightened her. On 30 September she arranged to stay with the Gibbins for a week. Archie, keen not to be left out, followed on and, as had become the pattern over the previous two years, he travelled across to her aunt's house most days by train. The Gibbins, like many other families at this time, had taken in a lodger, Albert Saunders, a young labourer. Engaged to be married, he was living in Attleborough only until his wedding. Annie liked him and whenever possible enjoyed his company. Archie on the other hand decided these occasional conversations the two had were a little too deep and meaningful. Jealous that she was paying Saunders more attention than he deserved, he confronted her and the two had a row. Annie later told her aunt

Baptist church at Sutton-in-the-Elms. The author

The old church at Croft. The author

that he had threatened violence and for the first time in their long relationship she felt a sense of fear. Archie, perhaps realising that he had gone too far, apologised and over the next two or three days they appeared to be on better terms. Annie had seemingly forgiven Archie his outburst and decided his threats were no more than hot air. But on Sunday 6 October his sense of jealousy reared its head once more. Having taken a train back to Attleborough with his good friend Leonard Hunt the two went to church to try and meet up with Annie, whom they knew would be attending morning service. When they arrived it was to find Annie already seated in the congregation with her aunt and uncle and beside her the Gibbins' lodger. Incensed at what he believed was nothing less than an act of betrayal, he ignored the couple after the service and told

Annie's uncle, Thomas Gibbins, once they were outside the church that he intended to leave the area for good. The two men then walked alone for a while, the elder giving the younger the benefit of his years and therefore his experience. He told Archie to forget about Annie. He was young, he should find someone else, the type of advice he thought would be well received. On the face of it Archie seemed to agree. Certainly he listened, chimed in with the odd point of his own and generally appeared to concur with the advice he was given. But it was all a sham; Archie was totally consumed by jealousy and somewhere deep inside he wanted revenge.

On the following day Annie caught the 11.45 morning train to Croft, as Archie had suspected she would. Thomas Gibbins had indicated to him the previous day that she intended to go

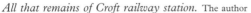

All that remains of Croft railway station. The author

home and he knew the train timetable well. He was waiting outside the station when she stepped off the carriage. Their meeting was amiable enough; he made no threats and to all intents and purposes was the old Archie she had grown to love. Unfortunately for her, the further they walked the more his attitude changed. As they entered a narrow lane that ran from the little village to the Fosse Road, some half a mile from the railway station, he confronted her again over the lodger, Saunders, a man whose name he did not know. In fact not knowing the name caused him as much anguish as believing she had embarked upon a secret affair. The argument became fiercely heated, Archie demanding she confess. She in turn denied the accusation and told him that she hardly knew the man. Grabbing hold of her by the throat, Archie insisted she tell him the man's name. Annie refused, and so he strangled her on the road and pushed her body in the ditch that ran alongside. Before he left her he took a bundle of letters, all written from Annie to himself, and stuffed them in the top of her dress.

Understandably desperate to escape, he then made his way via the fields back to Croft discarding his braces, which broke, and his shirt collar, as he ran. Arriving at Moore's public house, which overlooked the main street, he then went in and ordered two glasses of ginger beer before walking back to the railway station and catching the half-past one train to Leicester.

Local clothier, William Herbert, discovered Annie's body an hour later as he drove along the same lane en route to Broughton Astley. A quick examination confirmed that she was dead and police were on the scene within the hour. The braces,

Mr Moore's public house as it is today. The author

the collar and all the letters were retrieved before the end of the afternoon and the police were left in no doubt who Annie's killer had been.

Meanwhile, Archie, beside himself with guilt, wandered around Leicester until about half-past six that night then returned to Croft intent on finding Annie's body and moving it. Of course when he reached the lane, which was after eleven o'clock at night, the body had already been removed. So, afraid to go home he walked north, slept rough and caught the early morning train to Rugby. By the end of the following day, possibly realising that he had nowhere to run, he returned home and surrendered himself to police.

Five days later seventeen-year-old Annie Haines was buried in the graveyard at Sutton-in-the-Elms amidst a huge crowd of mourners most of whom lined the streets then followed on behind the sad cortege to mass inside the gates of the small cemetery as the funeral service moved from inside the church to the graveside. She was two weeks away from what would have been her eighteenth birthday.

The inquest, held at Croft two days later, was somewhat of a foregone conclusion, with Archie in custody and admitting his guilt there was little more to be learned. Surgeon Montagu Gunning, who had carried out the post-mortem, told the coroner's court that there was no doubt about the killing being a case of murder. Indents around the neck were consistent with having been strangled and examination of the internal organs had confirmed death by asphyxiation. A variety of other witnesses took the stand to tell how Archie had been seen around Croft on the morning of the murder prior to Annie's train arriving at the station, and others were able to confirm some of his movements after the discovery of the woman's body in the ditch. Added to this was a notebook entry read to the court by police sergeant Stapleton, which detailed Archie's guilt recorded shortly after his arrest:

I am sorry now I done it. I strangled her with one hand, and she was dead in about three minutes, and I laid her in the ditch. She was with another young man on Sunday night, and I asked her his name, and she refused to tell me.

Coroner Mr Bouskell had little choice but to return a verdict of wilful murder.

Archibald Page appeared before Leicestershire magistrates a week later and after a brief hearing was ordered to stand trial at the autumn assizes. The trial itself opened on 29 October at the Castle, Leicester. People had been queuing for hours to gain entry and by the time the judge took his seat there were no spaces left in which to either stand or sit. Archie, dressed in a dark suit, was reported by the *Leicester Daily Mercury* to appear fairly self-possessed and in rude good health. When clerk of the court, a Mr Coleridge, stood to face him as he read out the formal charge, Archie gripped the rail that ran around the top of the dock and in a clear voice pleaded not guilty.

Barrister Ryland Atkins, MP, ably assisted by Bernard Campion, both extremely successful Crown prosecutors, opened the case with a lengthy speech to the jurors outlining the events of 7 October. Using letters retrieved from Annie's body he then proceeded to tell her story in her own words. Reading out extracts from the earlier letters to illustrate how she had loved Archie and then from those most recent that showed a depth of concern over his growing jealousy, ending with words from her final letter that proved too poignant for some of those in court:

> *... I love you dearly still and I shall go with no one else but you ... May God forgive you for saying I have been going with another chap when I have not ... I can not see what I am writing, for my eyes are full of bitter tears ... I shall be your lover to the death ...*

He then proceeded to read in full a short letter that had been retrieved from Archie's jacket pocket upon his arrest. A letter, claimed Ryland Atkins, which had been penned before the murder:

Oct 7 1907

A Lovers Crime

May heaven forgive me for what I have done. But we are both ready to die together for our lives is not worth living, for our plan is to die together, but now I have killed my own sweetheart. I cannot die myself, but I will give the police a bit of work to chat (catch) the handcuff king. But they have got a champion wrestler before there own eyes, but chat him if you can, but by the time this letter is found I shall be over 100 miles away in Somersetshire: but I am well known all over England for my cleaver work, but my madles (medals), I have gave them away. So now I must enclose my short farewell letter.

A. E. Page
The handcuff
King
Goodbye
Lass.

Despite the bad grammar and poor spelling it was damning in the extreme. As Ryland Atkins pointed out, the medals referred to were won by Archie for his ability to demonstrate skills at First Aid, which, he pointed out, meant that the young man had a comprehensive knowledge of the human body and its vulnerable points. Archie, he claimed, knew exactly where to position his hand in order to effect strangulation, and the fact that the killing was done using only the left hand showed all too clearly that he was equally adept at locating those vulnerable points.

THE ACCUSED
(ARCHIBALD PAGE)

From the outset it was going to be extremely difficult to defend a charge of murder when the evidence was apparently so clear and irrefutable. The defence case, therefore, was forced to go along lines of insanity or accidental death. In other words was Archie mad at the time he carried out the killing or did

Archie Page. Leicester Mercury

Annie die more from shock than his actions? In the case of the latter the accidental premise was totally destroyed when Dr Gunning, who had presented his facts at the inquest, reiterated his medical findings but with some additional detail. He refuted the defence argument that Annie could have died from any other cause other than violence. According to his testimony all the relevant internal organs were healthy and, after detailing his findings for each to the court, he added that not a single injury sustained by the dead woman could be attributed to either shock or accident. The young woman, he insisted, had died as a direct result of applied force to the throat by a man that understood just where applied pressure would prove fatal.

Undaunted, the defence team then shifted toward insanity, the obvious and probably only realistic avenue open to them. But even here they found the door to diminished responsibility firmly closed against them. Despite the knowledge that Archie had an aged uncle, George Sawbridge, safely locked away in Leicester County Asylum, they were unable to prove any sort of medical link. Dr Moore, surgeon at Leicester prison, testified that having had Archie under close observation since his arrest he had exhibited no symptoms of mental incapacity, rather the opposite. Despite hostile questioning, Dr Moore stoically resisted all attempts to force a change in his assessment insisting that in his expert opinion, Archibald Page was perfectly sane when he committed murder. A second doctor, brought to court by the prosecution from the same asylum in which Archie's uncle resided, offered up corroborating testimony. Again and under fierce questioning from the defence counsel, he refused to bend when it came to his opinion of Archie's sanity. When the murder took place, he told the hushed court, there could be no doubt whatsoever that he was completely sane when he attacked Annie Haines, furthermore, he added, during his own examinations carried out over three consecutive days he fully concurred with Dr Moore's assessment that there were absolutely no indicators to suggest anything other than complete sanity.

The final, and ultimately most damning piece of evidence, then came to light when the prosecuting counsel read out the statement Archie had made to police in admission of his guilt:

I have been going out with my girl, Annie Elizabeth Haines, for about two years. We have always been good friends, and I have been over to Hinckley to see her two or three times a week. I did not like it on Friday, when I waited outside the house where she was stopping at Attleborough from six to half past eight, when she did not come out ... When I called to see her on last Sunday night I got fair jealous. I was along with my mate, a chap named Hunt, and saw Gibbins and his wife, and my girl and the lodger at the chapel. The lodger kept staring at us ... We waited about and saw them come out of the chapel. My girl and the lodger were walking in front and Gibbins and his missus were walking behind. I spoke to Gibbins ... My girl was coming to shake hands and bid me good night but the lodger called her back.

On Monday morning I wrote a letter, which I kept in my pocket, and which was taken from me by the policeman who searched me ... Knowing my girl was going home before dinner time I thought I would meet her at Croft, and get to know the lodger's name and why she was walking about with him ... I met her about three hundred yards from Croft station ... I walked with her about 150 yards (115 metres) *towards Broughton and asked her several times to tell me the name of the lodger, and how it was she was walking out with him ... She said, ' it is nothing to do with you.' I said if you don't tell me I will take jolly good care that you won't see him again. I then took hold of her with my left hand at her back and my right hand at her breast, and pushed her back on the side of the road. I said, Annie what is the lodger's name? She said, ' It's nowt to do with you.' I then lifted her into the dyke and placed my left hand round her windpipe and kept it there while some men from the quarry went by on their bikes ... She did not try to get away; she put her hand on my face once. When I took my hand off her throat I found she was dead. ... I stood in the ditch for a minute or two and took the letters out of my pocket and put them under her jacket, kissed her hands and face and left.*

It was as incontrovertible as it was no doubt accurate and meant for young Archie Page that there was to be no mitigation in his defence that could be acceptable to a jury. As the trial drew to a close the judge, in his summing up, told the jurors they were not to shirk from their duty. This one single statement, he told them, had simplified the case and made the circumstances surrounding the murder simple enough to understand. As far as insanity was concerned he pointed out the lack of evidence in support of the supposition:

> *Every person was supposed to be sane until he had shown that he was insane. It was not for the prosecution in this case to prove this man's sanity. If the defence was set up that he was irresponsible in law, it was for the defence to show, by evidence on which the jury could rely, that he was not responsible. Unless it could be shown that at the time of the act he was not in a mental condition to be able to understand the nature and quality of what he was doing, he must be held to be sane.*

It was a valid point and one that had been more than proven throughout the trial. There was no doubt whatsoever that Archie was sane, as confirmed by medical opinion. There was equally no doubt that he had been the man that had strangled Annie Haines. Motive was simple jealousy; Archie's misguided belief that his girlfriend had been having an affair of sorts with another man had cost her dearly. Perhaps more than he had intended but there was only one certainty and that was his guilt. For the jury their verdict was, to all intents and purposes, a foregone conclusion and after an adjournment of only ten minutes they pronounced him guilty. He was duly sentenced to death.

But Archibald Ernest Page had one thing on his side and that was age. Both he and Annie were extremely young in the eyes of the law and the minute the verdict was announced moves were afoot to attempt a review of the verdict. The argument mounted by the defence after the trial was not that he was either innocent or mentally incapable, it was that he was too young to die on the gallows at Leicester. The judge, after pronouncing the sentence, had indicated that a recommendation to mercy would be forwarded to the appropriate authorities. This gave a glimmer of hope to those that earnestly believed he ought to be spared because of his youth and a vigorous campaign was mounted. There was sympathy in the city, some believing that he had been too young to realise his actions, others that it could not possibly have been intentional murder. Either way, people were prepared to support the plea for clemency. From Archie, according to reports, there seemed little interest. He had expressed no real concern when the court had passed sentence and had given the appearance of a man in agreement with the verdict. Whether that was so is not known but certainly the Home Office took the view that whatever his crime the hand of mercy should be extended. A reprieve was finally granted and received by Leicester prison authorities on 12 November, just prior to the scheduled execution date, commuting the sentence to one of penal servitude for life.

CHAPTER 12

The Death of a Prizefighter
The Killing of Frederick Greaves
1911

...James raised the gun to his shoulder and fired once.

It could be said of twenty-six-year-old James Stevens that life had been tough since his marriage to Annie in January of 1909. Certainly on a work front it had been extremely hard. Since leaving the army he had found employment difficult to come by and even harder to keep a hold of once found. Taking work, like thousands of others, in the shoe trade ought to have brought employment for life but like many other industries there were peaks and troughs. For the whole of his short marriage it seemed to him that the industry had been in one of those troughs and that he had suffered because of it.

In September of 1910 his wife had given birth to their first child, a boy. It ought to have been a cause for celebration but with money in short supply it became the cause of nothing but friction. Struggling to make ends meet and with an additional mouth to feed, Annie, the only skilled worker of the two, was forced back to work within weeks of the birth. Machinists were highly sought after and for her there was never likely to be a lack of full time work. For James it was exactly the opposite. With no key skills it was always he that was forced out of work whenever the industry cut back its workforce. In April 1911, after only a few weeks of general labouring he found himself, yet again, in the all too familiar situation of trying to find a new job after being made redundant for the umpteenth time. By now the strain was beginning to tell on the couple. Being

Leicester c.1900. Author's collection

severely handicapped financially for so long had brought inevitable repercussions. For the Stevens family nothing was ever affordable, with only one income coming into the house and with no sign of any improvement within the near future the couple finally split. Desperate to change things, James decided that there was little alternative and so all their belongings were sold, the proceeds equally divided between the two and Annie sent off with the baby to take lodgings with the King family at 21 Bow Street, Leicester. James got on his bike, literally, and went off in search of permanent work. Cycling first to Kettering, where a cousin offered him a bed for a few weeks, he then cycled around the south of the country in search of work. With Kettering as a base, situated as it was within the heart of the shoe industry, the house afforded him an opportunity to travel around Northamptonshire where he earnestly believed work would be made available to him. He was very wrong. In May 1911 industry generally was not having the best of years and despite his optimism, and his age, he was met with rejection at every turn. After a fruitless sixty-two mile cycle ride into East Anglia, where he had been told of a company taking on workers, he decided to return to Leicester.

On Saturday afternoon, 13 May, he arrived at Annie's lodgings in Bow Street in need of a little sympathy and understanding, instead of which he found his son in the hands of a baby-minder and his wife in *The Three Cranes* on Humberstone Road. After a brief conversation with the Kings, who sublet a room to his wife, he determined to bring her back to look after the baby. Incensed by what he saw as her callous indifference to his own plight and an uncaring attitude toward their baby, there was little doubt as to his state of mind when he walked in through the doors of *The Three Cranes* smoking room. Annie, who had been drinking for some three hours by the time he arrived, was sitting with her brother, Fred Greaves, and his wife, Alice, and she had no intention of leaving. To his credit, and despite his anger, James made no show of his disappointment in her or made any public demand that she return home. Instead, preferring to take a more diplomatic approach, he pulled up a stool, sat down and tried to talk to her. But Annie was in no mood to listen, buoyed up by the alcohol and with a week's wage in her pocket, nothing he could say was about to change her plans for the rest of the afternoon. So, perhaps

The Three Cranes, *Leicester.* The author

believing diplomacy only stood any chance if he joined her, he accepted a proffered glass of beer and stayed. But it was not long before it became clear to those that shared the table that he was not about to relax and give up his day. Plainly he wanted his wife to go home and his attempt at suppressing his anger had only worked to a certain degree. One look at his face told those around him that all was not well. Eventually, after about an hour, he decided that he had had enough; in a whispered exchange between the two he told her he was off back to Bow Street and that he expected her to follow. She, of course, refused but brother-in-law Fred, who witnessed this brief debate, told his wife Alice to take Annie in hand and go after him.

The two women met with James in Wharf Street where he had stopped to talk to a Mrs Stanyon, the baby-minder he had met earlier in the afternoon. She was pushing his son in a pram toward the pub and he wanted her to take him back to the lodgings at Bow Street. When Annie came across the pair she insisted that James leave the baby with her and stooping down she scooped the child into her arms and told him she would

Wharf Street, Leicester today. The author

take him to her brother Fred's house. James snatched him back and after an exchange of words over her ability to care for the child in her drunken state he ran off. Unconcerned, Annie and sister-in-law Alice refused to follow on and merely carried on as if nothing had happened. James arrived at her lodgings some minutes later, deposited the boy with the Kings and then ran back up toward Wharf Street. With only one intention, and without warning, he ran straight toward his wife and stabbed her in the neck. In a moment of understandable panic Alice lunged at him in an attempt to fend him off and in a brief, one-sided struggle, was slashed across her face before James managed to effect his escape. Annie was extremely lucky, the knife failed to penetrate to any serious depth, otherwise she would quite possibly have died on the street. As it was she was taken by neighbours to hospital and alongside Alice had her wound stitched. On being discharged, and not wanting to return to her lodgings for fear of a further attack, she returned with Alice to her brother's house at 180 Argyle Street.

James, meanwhile, had run off to a friend's house on Mansfield Road. Well aware that his attempt at killing his wife had failed and keen to complete the job he had started he managed successfully to talk his friend, Harry Norman, into loaning him a rifle. Spinning a web of lies about going shoot-ing the following morning he convinced Norman that he had planned to do a bit of poaching. All too well aware of how money had been hard to come by for his friend and food expensive, Norman took little persuading and agreed to the loan. But, of course, James had no intention of shooting rabbits. Well aware of where his wife would have gone he made straight for the house on Argyle Street.

When he arrived the front door was already open to the street and following young Joseph Emerton, whose mother had chosen that night to visit the Greaves family, he walked straight in behind the boy. Pandemonium broke out the minute the gun was seen and in a momentary loss of nerve James turned tail and ran. But he did not run far. Once back out in the street he stopped to catch his breath whilst he plucked up the courage to return a second time. It was at that precise moment that Fred Greaves, alerted by his wife Alice's shouts ran out through the front door to confront him. Without a moment's hesitation James raised the gun to his shoulder and fired once. Fred fell dead on his face.

If, at that moment, he had intended to escape it was already too late. As the fatal shot was fired Police Constable Clarke, who had been alerted earlier about a man carrying a gun, turned the corner at the bottom of the street. Unable to prevent the shooting he nevertheless witnessed it, made the arrest and discovered fifty-nine additional cartridges in James Stevens' jacket pocket. There was no doubt he had intended to fire off more than one shot if need be and in a later statement was unequivocal about his intentions. Annie had been lucky for a second time that night.

Frederick Greaves was only thirty years old. The two men had known each other as friends for only two years but others had known him from his hard won reputation in the boxing ring. A modern-day prizefighter, he had fought some reputable boxers in his earlier days and was well known around Leicester after having boxed at the *Old Mafeking* some years earlier in an epic fight against local hero Percy Sherriff, for a purse of £59, a fight he lost after being knocked out. Why did James kill him? Probably more of a reflex action than a deliberate attempt to commit murder, Greaves was certainly not involved with his wife, nor had there been any arguments or disputes between the two men. James, in fact, was at a loss to explain why he had pulled the trigger when he did, all he seemed able to do was apologise.

Interest and curiosity therefore, brought the crowds to Leicester when his trial eventually opened on 13 June before Mr Justice Pickford and the Crown Court was packed to capacity. Stevens, having had a month to contemplate his fate, had still not been able to offer up any reason for the murder nor had police uncovered any motive. Entering a plea of not guilty, he took his place in the dock and, according to the *Leicester Daily Mercury*, was outwardly calm as he took his seat to listen to the prosecution outline their case to the court. Straight-forward and incontrovertible, was how they presented their argument to the jury. James Stevens, who had never denied the killing, nor could he, had simply shot the wrong person. On the

London Road, Leicester c.1930. Author's collection

night of the killing Greaves had been mistaken for his own wife, it was dark, very late and as he pointed the gun he was extremely angry. When his finger pressed the trigger he, the prosecution insisted, believed that he was about to kill his wife who was the cause of all his mental anguish. It was a powerful and quite probably accurate assessment of the facts and James Stevens state of mind. It was also damning, particularly when the rider was added that because Steven's had admitted intending to murder his wife then any argument in favour of accidental shooting was fatally flawed. It could not have been accidental if murder had always been the intent.

The defence, all too well aware of this fact and ably led by Mr Everard, made no attempt to mount a defensive argument along those grounds. Instead they accepted that Stevens was guilty and that he had borrowed the gun with the express intention of killing Annie, but, they argued, he had done so when the state of his mind was unhinged. The shooting of Greaves, they maintained, was therefore accidental or at least unintentional, but having accepted and acknowledged in statements made after his arrest that he had always intended to use the weapon meant he must also accept a degree of culpability.

Blameworthy certainly, but not guilty of murder, when James Stevens had fired at the figure emerging from the dark it had happened almost as a reflex action. There was never, they continued to argue, any premeditation about the act, therefore, murder as a charge had no foundation in fact.

There was no doubting the sincerity or logic behind the defence's reasoning and in his summing up at the end of the day's proceedings Mr Justice Pickford expanded upon the point of law they had raised:

> *If he had shot the woman it would have been very difficult to say that it was not as deliberate a case of murder as they could have. They must not say, however, that it was murder in this case because if he had shot his wife it would only then have been murder ... They could only say the prisoner was not guilty if he could convince them that when he fired at Greaves he was in danger of death or some very serious bodily harm indeed. Nothing would excuse the use of a deadly weapon but that prospect. If one were in danger merely of getting what was called a hammering, he was not justified in using the weapon, but it might be sufficient provocation, if the jury thought it was, to reduce the crime from murder to manslaughter.*

Knowing Greaves' boxing background meant that the jury accepted unanimously that had James Stevens not fired when he did that the ex-boxer could have done him some serious physical damage. This hypothesis was without any evidence that Greaves had intended any harm when he came running out of the front door of his house. Nevertheless it saved Stevens' life. After an adjournment of thirty-five minutes they returned a manslaughter verdict and he was sentenced to seven years' penal servitude.

CHAPTER 13

The Threepenny Bit Killer
The Murder of Ann Harris
1911

But he was not going to the scaffold quietly...

Seventy-five-year-old Ann Harris had lived alone in a small cottage on the edge of Walcote village, some two miles outside Lutterworth, since the death of her husband in 1901. She lived a frugal life though it is fair to say her needs were small and with her sister living close by, company was never in short supply. Neither was money. A domestic servant for most of her working life, she had developed the habit of saving many years earlier and had successfully put by a small nest egg that supported her in her retirement. As well as this small amount of capital she had also saved a significant number of silver threepenny bits. Accumulated over the latter years of her life, the coins were kept in purses locked away in a chest of drawers in her bedroom. Alongside these she also kept

The tiny village of Walcote today. The author

a gold watch that she had bought some thirty years earlier, a gold chain and a number of half sovereigns. It was common knowledge to those that knew her, not that anyone ever saw the collection, more that she had never made a secret of its existence as any of her previous employers would have been able to testify. Neither did she hide the fact that her eyesight had been failing, and that she had been forced to use an old magnifying glass whenever she needed to read. Callers at the house had grown used to her frailties and her sister Sarah, because of the difficulties with her sight, had begun calling at nine o'clock each morning to help her make breakfast.

For Ann it was a welcome start to her day and no doubt an opportunity to catch up with village news and gossip. Sarah seemed willing enough to carry out the chore and after sorting out breakfast would often then spend much of the morning pottering around the cottage and generally ensuring her sister was set for the rest of the day. So when she arrived at her usual time on 25 January 1911 there was nothing to suggest the day's routine would be any different to those she had grown accustomed to over the previous weeks. But the horror that awaited her as she turned her key in the lock would change her life forever.

Ann Harris had been attacked during the night and her body lay at the bottom of the stairs. She had been strangled; the length of bandage used to kill her was still tightly wound around her neck. She had also been tied to a chair, which lay on top of her and to which she was still secured. The upstairs room in which she had slept had been ransacked. A poker lay on top of the chest of drawers beside her bed and had been used to prise open the drawer locks. Three purses lay discarded on the floor. Two were empty and one held a couple of sovereigns. In one of the drawers were found forty-three silver threepenny bits, but the gold watch, gold chain and her magnifying glass were all missing. A later post-mortem revealed that she had also sustained six broken ribs and severe bruising around the chest area indicating that her killer had knelt on her to carry out the strangulation.

The first policeman on the scene, Sergeant Stapleton, found that the front door had been forced, the lock being almost broken away. He also found that the bed had been slept in, suggesting that the old lady had been disturbed by the thief, and more than likely gone downstairs to investigate a noise. The chair had come from the kitchen and none of her injuries were consistent with having been pushed down stairs so it was presumed she had been beaten and strangled where she had been found. Nothing else in the house appeared to have been touched. After listening to neighbour Elizabeth Gibson whose house overlooked the yard at the back of Ann Harris's house, a yard known locally as Voss's Yard, the police sergeant made a thorough examination of the ground around the doorway. According to Mrs Gibson, at around midnight she had been disturbed by a series of loud noises outside. When she had drawn back her curtains she had seen a man stooping down below Ann Harris's door as if examining the lock. Unable to see him clearly in the dark she had watched as he struck first one match and then a second in an attempt to light up the doorway. The light from these was enough for her to distinguish certain features. She told the sergeant that the man she had seen was stoutly built, bulky around the shoulders and with a distinctive moustache. Furthermore, he had a face she believed she would be able to identify again. After apparently failing to open the door, she told the policeman she had continued to watch as he then entered Ann Harris's coalhouse and there struck up another match, which briefly lit up the window. At that point she had gone downstairs to check her own locks and by the time she had returned to her bedroom window the man, whoever he was, had gone. The matches were found where they had been cast down and within hours the description, despite its vagueness, had been matched against a man seen in Lutterworth during the evening of the murder. That man was William Henry Palmer.

A painter by trade, Palmer had been working in Manchester selling fish but had found himself unemployed at the beginning of January 1911. Short of money he had deliberately dressed himself in poor clothes and had 'gone on the tramp', as it was known. Intending to walk to London where he believed prospects would be better, armed with a pocket full of shoe-laces, which he sold door-to-door, and a hard luck story, which

The centre of Bitteswell village. The author

he used to beg money, he had set out a week earlier. On the afternoon of the murder he had arrived in the village of Bitteswell where he managed to convince Reverend Ward, vicar of the parish, that he was a sober man in need of help. The vicar, obviously a charitable man, gave him 2d. Palmer followed that by selling his laces round the village at $1\frac{1}{2}$d a pair, which he did successfully and before nightfall had arrived in Lutterworth. Here he booked himself into Dixon's Lodging House for the night but never slept in the room. Instead he went out drinking and after arriving back at the lodgings after 11 pm was refused admittance. Where he went between this time and seven o'clock the next morning is what caused the greatest amount of debate after his later arrest. Certainly when Lutterworth railway station opened its gates at 7 am he was there. After buying a ticket to London he travelled to Rugby where he was to change trains and walked into the *Great Central Hotel*. He stayed there for some time before making his way to the *Victoria Inn*, a short walk away and eventually setting out on foot toward Northampton. By the time he had arrived there police were already on his trail. Too many people with new laces had been able to identify him and their description of the badly dressed hawker was too close to that of Elizabeth Gibson for the investigating team to ignore. But they were not to catch up with him for a further three days during which time he had travelled to Charing Cross, London and then on to Folkestone,

Remnants of the old railway line into Lutterworth. The author

where he had claimed to be a fishmonger. Detective Inspector Taylor of Leicestershire Constabulary finally made the arrest at Tames Dining Rooms, Folkstone. Palmer, of course, denied all knowledge of the murder and insisted he had never been to Walcote in his life and there the mystery began.

In his initial statement to police Palmer told them he had gone straight from Lutterworth to London and on to Folkestone. He later amended his statement and said that he had walked from Lutterworth to Northampton and found a handkerchief by the roadside that had contained money, two sovereigns, a half sovereign and a number of two-shilling pieces. But in both statements he made no reference to Rugby. Police then began a thorough investigation as to his movements between the 24 and 25 January.

A not too difficult exercise to carry out because Palmer had never hidden his presence from anyone and selling laces along the way meant they were able to piece together a reasonably accurate plan of his movements. But Rugby did not initially figure in the enquiry. That only came about after a claim was received by police that he had sent a telegram from Rugby railway station to a house in Manchester. Further investigations then revealed the visits to the two public houses and one single damning fact. Edward Evans, the barman at the *Victoria Inn* who had served Palmer his drinks, told the officers that he distinctly remembered Palmer because he had paid for all the drinks with silver threepenny bits. According to Evans, Palmer had told him he was a drover travelling to Dover and had just been paid. By way of excuse he had added that his boss had only small change to give him and had asked for a bag to carry it all in, which Evans had been unable to supply. All damning stuff and when Elizabeth Gibson made a formal identification on 31 January police were satisfied that they had caught Ann Harris's killer.

Lutterworth Police Station. The author

Palmer continued to deny his involvement, insisting that had he committed a murder he would never have done something as stupid as visiting a pub and spending the proceeds of a robbery, particularly when those proceeds were silver threepenny bits. Furthermore, he continued to insist, Rugby was not even on his route to London. But the evidence was almost overwhelming. Enquiries in Lutterworth had found that on the night of the murder Palmer had visited several pubs in company with a woman. In each of these he had bought drinks and appeared not to be as hard up as he had claimed to those that bought his laces as he passed through the various villages en route. Though this was prior to the murder he had continued to visit a number of public houses throughout the next two days and in each had spent money. A calculation made by the investigating team estimated that his spend over two or three

days had been in the range of twelve shillings, a significant sum
for an out of work painter. But more incriminating was his use
of small change and in particular silver threepenny bits. These
he appeared to have used in all the pubs he had visited after the
murder but not before.

The trial opened before Mr Justice Pickford on 12 June, some
five months after his arrest, and Palmer, who had never changed
his claim of innocence, pleaded not guilty. From the outset
his defence team, ably led by Bernard Campion, set out their
assertion that the case was one of mistaken identity. Palmer,
they insisted, had been brought to court on the flimsiest of
evidence and absolutely nothing had been discovered at the
scene of the crime that put their client inside the house of Ann
Harris. A contentious point given the eyewitness testimony
from Elizabeth Gibson but one they believed had real credence.

Elizabeth Gibson in fact was amongst the first prosecution
witnesses to take the stand and one of the few to come under
intense scrutiny. In evidence she was forced to admit that
her seventy years of age had taken its toll upon her eyesight and
that her eyes were not as good as they had been. Campion
demanded to know how it was that despite these shortcomings
she had managed to identify a man from some thirty-six feet
away, on a dark night, with only the odd snatch of light from a
match and from behind. Stoically she stuck to the detail of her
original statement and argued that her sight had not failed to
such an extent she could no longer distinguish the features of a
man, particularly one caught by a light. But she was eventually
forced to concede that her identification was made less on facial
features and more on the man's build. Palmer of course was
a powerfully built man, but that, argued Campion, was not
sufficient reason to claim he had been the man seen on the
night Ann Harris was murdered. The first seeds of doubt had
been cast.

The second came in the defence claim that it was impossible
to claim that Palmer, or anyone else for that matter, had stolen
money from the Harris house because it was not known how
much money the old lady had owned. Neither had it been
known exactly how many silver sixpences had been in the
drawer of the bedroom. When forty-three had been found was

it not feasible, they argued, that none had been stolen? Because the precise number had never been known it was impossible to then claim that the killer had stolen an unspecified quantity and just because Palmer had spent such coins in a pub was not evidence of that theft. The defence went on to argue that the only items that could, with any safety, be attached to the murder were the gold watch, gold chain and the magnifying glass.

The third element of doubt they cast was in regard to the amount of money he had carried around with him. Police contention had been throughout the case that he had more cash to spend after the killing than before. But, maintained the defence, that seemed hardly true. The police's own investigations had revealed that he had never been a man on hard times despite his appearance or his door-to-door activities. This, they told the court, had been a deliberate attempt by Palmer to deceive. He needed people to believe he was poor if he was to raise money through begging and selling. But, as police investigations had revealed, he had spent money freely on the night of the murder and therefore there could be no doubt as to his financial state when he arrived in Lutterworth. To believe otherwise, they contended, was simply naive. It was also possibly naive to believe he would have had money in his pocket of higher denomination than a silver threepenny bit. The nature of begging is one that requires the public to spend their small change. No one, they argued, gives a beggar a half sovereign.

These were well-constructed points and ones not easily discredited. But the defence team had known when they made these points that one specific fact had been unearthed some nine days earlier that was set to fatally damage their case. The arguments they had raised had been intended to cast a net of doubt across Palmer's guilt, essentially a mechanism to lessen the impact of this key evidence in the eyes of the jury.

On 3 June police had decided to mount a thorough search of the *Great Central Hotel* at Rugby. Exactly what had suddenly caused them to revisit the place five months after their first visit made back in January was never explained. But inside one of the toilet cisterns in the men's toilet they discovered a gold watch, a gold chain and a magnifying glass in a gold frame. All the items were then identified as having been stolen from Ann Harris's house. Palmer, they were satisfied, had been drinking in the bar and so therefore had obviously placed them in the cistern. Possibly the most damning piece of evidence against him and one Bernard Campion knew he had to explain away.

The prosecution brought watchmaker, George Haswell, to the court and he told the jurors that in his expert opinion, having examined the watch that it had been in water for at least four to five months, much of the internal workings had gone rusty and it would have needed that amount of time for this build-up of rust to accumulate. Despite rigorous cross examination his testimony remained constant and so, ran the argument, if the jeweller was correct in his assessment of the water damage, Palmer had to have been the man who had put it into the cistern and if that were so then he had murdered Ann Harris.

This was the crucial point of the trial. Campion knew that if this evidence were allowed to stand unchallenged then his client would go to the gallows. In a desperate attempt to counter this he had brought to court a respected and well-known Leicester jeweller, Richard Gibson, in the hope that his local reputation would hold greater sway with the jury. In his testimony to the court he challenged the earlier findings. Rust, he claimed, would have formed within two or three days and had it been submerged for the amount of time claimed would have been far more extensive. Unfortunately for the defence team under cross-examination he was also forced to admit that he had never seen a watch that had been in water. It blew a hole through the defence strategy and caused irreparable damage.

Nevertheless, in the closing speeches at the end of the trial Campion made a valiant attempt to discredit the evidence discovered in the *Great Central* toilet block. Accepting that the items found had, without exception, all been stolen from the Harris house he mounted the argument that it made no sense for Palmer, had he been the killer, to hide them in a place he was never likely to return to. Nor was it beyond the realms of possibility that the real killer had placed them there after Palmer's arrest and in order to ensure he was convicted. It held no sway with the jury and after a seventy-two minute adjournment they returned a guilty verdict and Palmer was sentenced to death.

But he was not going to go to the scaffold quietly, continuing to insist that he was innocent he refused to leave his cell on the morning of his execution. John Ellis, Britain's executioner at this time, had arrived in Leicester twenty-four hours earlier to conduct the preliminaries, which was the normal routine. As a result of this he was aware that when he walked into the cell at a few minutes before 8 am on the 19 July there would be some resistance from his prisoner. What he could never have anticipated was just how great that resistance was to be. Accusing Ellis and the prison governor of murder Palmer refused to acknowledge his guilt and attacked the two men. It took ten prison officers to finally subdue him and hold him down before Ellis was able to pinion his hands behind his back. Ellis then wasted no time in taking Palmer from the cell and the execution was carried out with some haste to prevent any further violence.

Whether William Henry Palmer had murdered Ann Harris is obviously debatable. John Ellis however had no doubts about his guilt and discussed it at length in his book, *Diary of a Hangman*. What the jury at the trial never knew, according to Ellis, was that Palmer had been found guilty of murder some years earlier in South Africa for the brutal killing of a farmer. The sentence had been commuted because of his age, as he was only a teenager when the murder took place, and after serving a prison sentence he had been sent back to England. At the time of his arrest he was also wanted in connection with a Manchester murder in 1910 and there is no doubting that after he had left Lutterworth on 25 January he had a pocket full of silver threepenny bits.

CHAPTER 14

For The Sake of a Horse
The Murder of James Warren
1914

... they had stumbled across a murder scene.

In May 1914 the marriage between thirty-two-year-old Arnold and Ethel Warren was in its death throes. The couple, married by this time for eight years, had been in difficulties for some time. Yet, of course, in 1906 when the two had stood side by side in the church life was very different. An engineer by trade, Arnold had held down a good job and they had no serious financial worries. Their first child, a son named James, had been born in 1911 and had the marriage remained firm, no doubt there would have been others. But at around the same time Arnold began to supplement his income through gambling and the gambling medium he chose was horse racing. An avid fan, he believed ardently that he could raise more money through betting than he could through working. Initially there were successes, as there often are, and he bought the lie that he could change his life forever. But of course he was wrong and as time passed these successes became less and less frequent. By the start of 1914 he was in debt and the losses were mounting. Undaunted, Arnold continued to gamble often using money set aside for food and rent until at last his wife decided she had had enough. In May of that year the couple had a violent argument and Arnold struck her. It had been the first time he had ever shown a violent streak and for Ethel it would be the last. After issuing a summons against him she was awarded a separation and a court order demanding he pay a ten-shilling a week payment to help support herself and their son. It did little to restore the relationship and even less to warn Arnold away from the racetrack. What it did do was cause a level of irrational anger in Arnold that inflicted devastating consequences upon the tiny family two months later.

Forced to earn her own keep despite the ten-shilling support, Ethel took a job that required her to work five days a week. Like many women today, to facilitate this, she also needed childcare for their son, three-year-old James. Fortunately for Ethel the marriage breakdown had not soured the relationship between herself and Arnold's mother, Mary, who agreed to take on the rôle. So, before Ethel went off to work each day, she arranged for eleven-year-old Edith Skidmore to collect the little boy in his pram and push him the short distance to Mary's house at 48 Gaul Street, Leicester. Edith then collected him at the end of the day and pushed him back home. It was an arrangement that worked well. It was also an arrangement that Arnold monitored carefully, not because he mistrusted his wife but because he intended to seize his son. There was no altruistic reason for taking his son away, just a simple intent to murder the boy.

Arnold, unable to control his gambling habit, and riven by a range of emotions that tended to veer from jealousy to inexplicable anger, wanted to exact revenge. That revenge he

Clock Tower, Leicester c.1910. Author's collection

had decided would manifest itself in the murder of his son and then his own suicide. The twin deaths he believed would then be seen as just retribution against the wife he considered had deserted him without due cause. Perverse and depraved in the extreme but to his mind at that time an effective and very personal revenge, his opportunity arrived on 10 July.

After pocketing all the money he owned he bought himself a bottle of poison and placed the rest as a bet on a horse, *Early Hope*, running at Haydock. He then went in search of his wife. The two met at the clock tower at Humberstone Gate. Flourishing a blue bottle in front of her face he told her candidly of what he had done adding the rider that if the horse lost he would kill himself. Ethel believed none of it. She had grown used to histrionics over the last few years and believed his threat of suicide to be no more than an attention-seeking outburst: she was very wrong. The horse, of course, lost.

At half-past five that same evening Arnold, now penniless, laid in wait by the swings at the Fosse Road Recreation Ground. This was the place he knew young Edith Skidmore would pass by en route back to his wife's lodgings with his son. It had become her habit to take the little boy on a walk before returning him home and like thousands of other children swings were irresistible to him. With no reason to fear the boy's

Humberstone Gate, Leicester today. The author

father she made straight for him the moment she saw him sitting on the grass. The two talked for a while and then Arnold, without causing her any concern, gave her a note. He told her to take it to his mother's house on Gaul Street whilst he played with James on the swings. She readily agreed and ran off leaving father and son together. When she returned some half an hour later the two had gone.

At around 8 pm Stanley Hackney was out walking with his girlfriend and saw what he at first thought to be a courting couple laying together on the grass. Curious as to whom they were, the pair walked a little closer and as they did so realised

The Clock Tower as it looks today. The author

they had stumbled across a murder scene. The child James Warren had been wickedly slashed about the throat with a cut-throat razor, his clothing and much of the ground around where he lay, saturated with blood. His father, Arnold, lay across him, unmarked as far as they could tell but clutching a small blue bottle in his right hand. Police arrived within minutes of the alarm being raised and after a quick check for vital signs found the unfortunate Arnold to be still alive. The poison had been laudanum and ineffective, rendering him unconscious but causing no lasting damage. Constable Ashburner, first policeman to arrive, quickly revived him and promptly arrested him for murder. At the police station two letters were found in his jacket, one addressed to his employer:

Just a last line to you. When you have the misfortune to employ a man who has a fall, take my tip and don't sleer over it, for if you had not thrown it at me I should still have been in your employ, but now I am what is called by some men a wastrel, and in a short time from now a murderer and suicide.

A second addressed simply enough, to whom it may concern:

These are the last words of one who, having had the best of chances any man could have, has persistently refused to take advantage of them and now tells of his last thoughts on looking into his past life, not dreading the future. I know I shall be better off, because my life has been one long series of mistakes, independence of masters, ignoring my mother's and wife's advice and going dead against my parents. I have now come to the last of all, a gambler's end, forsaken by my wife and child through my own fault.

Neither made a great deal of sense but perhaps this was a good indicator of his state of mind, though when fully recovered he made no attempt to excuse his actions. In an interview with Leicester's Superintendent Bowley a few hours after his arrival at Leicester Police Station he was very forthright, insisting that he had planned to commit the murder and had no regrets for doing so:

Narborough Road, Leicester c.1915. Author's collection

> *. . . I can't do anything else but plead guilty. I am straight enough there; it's correct. I went out with the firm intention to do it at dinner time. I had made a big bet today on* **Early Hope**, *running at Haydock Park and if it lost of doing myself in. I heard it had lost, and I went to the Park, the Fosse Recreation Ground, and lay down there and saw my boy Jim with a girl named Edith. I sent her away with a note as it suddenly struck me I would do away with the child as well as myself, with the idea of getting my own back with my wife . . .*

Midland Station, Leicester, c.1925. Author's collection

It was a damning statement and one from which he never veered, accepting of his own guilt and always insisting he had done it to spite his wife.

At his trial, which opened on 23 October 1914 his defending counsel, a Mr Disney, used the only defence available to him, that of insanity. He argued strongly that at the time Arnold Warren cut his son's throat he was not mentally capable of discerning right from wrong. Gambling, the break-up from his wife and a court appearance for domestic violence back in May had all been contributory factors in his mental decline. Therefore, he maintained, murder was an inappropriate charge and made no allowance for his state of mind at the time of the killing. It was a valiant attempt to deflect justice and would perhaps have held some validity had it not been for Mr Justice Avory who counselled that had Warren been mentally unhinged he would not have realised the severity of the crime he had committed. Arnold, he told the jurors, knew exactly what he had done and confessed in detail, which meant that he knew well enough his own actions and those were the actions of a murderer. The jury agreed and returned a guilty verdict. Arnold Warren was executed three weeks later at Leicester by hangman John Ellis.

The Green Bicycle Mystery
The Murder of Annie 'Bella'
Wright
1919

... with so much blood ... he [Constable Hill] refused to accept that Bella's death could be ... a cycling accident.

robably one of Britain's most baffling murders, forever known as the green bicycle murder, took place on the outskirts of Little Stretton in South Leicestershire on 5 July 1919. Twenty-two-year-old Annie Wright, 'Bella' to those who knew her, set out from her parents' house at Stoughton at half-past six that night to cycle to the nearby village of Evington. She had spent the afternoon writing letters and wanted to catch the post. The day was fine and warm, the post office at Evington only a couple of miles away and Bella was an accomplished cyclist. From Evington, which lies to the north west of Stoughton, she then cycled back past her home

The road out of Stoughton taken by 'Bella'. The author

on the outskirts of the village and on toward her uncle's house in the village of Gaulby. At some point on that journey a fellow cyclist joined her, a man she later claimed not to know, who told her he had travelled from Great Glen. Seemingly unperturbed by her new companion the two cycled on together reaching Gaulby at 7.15 pm. Here the two parted but the stranger on the green bicycle stayed on the village street for the next hour and a quarter.

The uncle, George Measures, had guests down that week-end, nephew James and his wife Mary. The pair had travelled south from Maltby near Rotherham and it is likely that Bella had chosen to cycle the extra distance to see them before they returned. All three watched the pair arrive and, not recognising the man, were obviously intrigued as to his identity. Bella had last been at the house just after Easter and on that occasion had brought with her a sailor, a man everyone in the family knew about, and a man they all believed she was likely to marry. So, when the stranger on the bicycle arrived there followed a flurry of questions. But Bella simply pushed them aside, insisting she had never met him before that afternoon, did not even know his name and had simply cycled alongside him for company. Seemingly unconcerned and possibly flattered by his interest in her she paid little attention to the fact that he did not cycle on

The small hamlet of Gaulby. The author

but stayed outside in the street. In fact Mary, who kept a watchful eye from the kitchen window, was more concerned than she. Keen to know more about the stranger she even asked her husband to go out and talk to him. All too willing to oblige, James, a keen cyclist himself and extremely knowledgeable about bicycles, had already noticed that the man was riding a BSA but of a type he had never seen before. Apart from being green it had a strange braking mechanism on the back wheel and with an insatiable appetite for all things mechanical James wanted to know how the system worked. But the man was not very forthcoming, unwilling or unable to explain the finer workings of his cycle and he proved difficult to converse with. So, apart from his high-pitched voice and cockney accent James uncovered nothing about the bike and even less about its rider, except one very salient fact. When his cousin finally re-emerged from the house, a little after 8.30 pm, he distinctly heard the man greet her using her name, Bella.

Setting out on the road toward Kings Norton he then watched the pair cycle off expecting that from there she would take the Stoughton road. It was the obvious and most direct route for her to take if she was to get home before dark. But for some reason never explained, Bella did no such thing. Instead, she cycled on through Kings Norton village, passing the Stoughton road junction probably intending to turn right onto the narrow road that would take her to Little Stretton. An odd and circuitous route to choose, certainly it would have added time to her journey, which considering the time of day was unnecessary but more importantly it also took her toward Great Glen. It also took her toward her own death. Her body was discovered at 9.20 pm, on the edge of Little Stretton village, on Gartrue Lane.

When farmer Joseph Cowell turned his herd of cattle onto the road he saw the body some 200 metres or so ahead of him. Bella lay in the road, her head toward its centre and her feet toward the left hand grass verge. She lay on her left side with her bicycle beside her, also on its left side, its front wheel pointing toward the village. She was dead but her body was still very warm. Blood had pooled around the head and she was still bleeding profusely. In the adjacent field near to a farm gate some few yards away lay a dead crow and a trail of bloody claw prints from Bella's body to the top of the gate from which the bird had fallen.

After a cursory examination for signs of life Cowell then picked her up in his arms and carried her from where she lay to the grass verge. This verge, nine feet (2.8 metres) wide, bordered both sides of the road and ran for a considerable distance beneath hedgerows some eight feet (2.5 metres) in height. Leaving her there he went off toward his farm from where he telephoned Dr E K Williams at his home in Billesdon and told him what he had found. The doctor, seemingly without any haste, arrived at the scene at 11.15 pm. Bella had by this time been lifted from where she had lain on the grassy verge and placed inside a milk float. Believing that it had simply been a cycling accident, he had the body taken to a nearby empty farm house and there, by the light of a candle, made a perfunctory examination after which he declared himself satisfied that she had died as a result of a fall and estimated time of death as having occurred some two hours earlier.

Watching all this with a growing sense of unease was Constable Hill, the first policeman on the scene; with so much blood lying in the road he refused to accept that Bella's death

The narrow road to Stretton. The author

could be attributed to a simple cycling accident. At 6 am on the following morning (Sunday) he walked back to the stretch of road where the body had been found and began a search. Hill began that search with the belief, unsubstantiated though it was, that Bella had been shot dead. To Hill's mind it was the only explanation that would explain the heavy loss of blood and if he were right, he knew there was a strong possibility that the spent bullet lay somewhere on that road. Finding it along such an expanse of open roadway was never going to be easy, but Hill was a determined man. Undaunted by his initial lack of early success he decided by late morning to take his suspicions back to his local office and pass them on to County Constabulary Headquarters at Leicester. There he received a sympathetic ear and after some debate it was agreed that they would send out a number of officers to do as thorough a ground search of the area as was possible. Success finally came at half past seven that night after a whole day of painstakingly slow searching and it was Hill himself that made the breakthrough. The bullet, a .45 calibre shell, he finally discovered embedded in earth some $17\frac{1}{2}$ feet (5.5 metres) from where the body had lain. Elated by the find he then walked back to the cottage where Bella's body still lay and wiped away the blood from her face. The puncture wound he knew had to exist became instantly visible, an inch behind and half an inch below the left eye.

Dr Williams was called out again from his Billesdon home to confirm the new findings, which he did, and after a little careful probing found that the wound extended upwards, inwards and backwards inside the head, through the brain toward an exit wound on the right side of the back of the head at the base of the skull, this exit wound was $1\frac{1}{2}$ inches wide. There was also bruising all around the entry wound that measured just over 1 inch and inside this bruising were tiny metal fragments. Her left hand, left arm and left side of her face had also sustained scratches caused by gravel as she hit the road. According to the doctor, death had been near instantaneous and had been caused by a gunshot wound to the head. At that point the mysterious other cyclist became the only suspect in the case.

On Tuesday 8 July, a description of the man was widely circulated and also published in the *Leicester Daily Mercury*. This described Bella's cycling companion as being aged between thirty-five and forty years, height 5 ft 7 inches to 5 ft 9 inches, clean shaven, hair turning grey, wearing a grey suit, grey cap, light rainproof coat, black boots and talking with a high-pitched voice but inclined to be quiet and uncommunicative. The bicycle, which offered up the best opportunity of an arrest should he have continued to use it, was described as being green enamel, black mudguards, upturned handlebars, three speed gears and with the singularly most unusual feature of having a back pedalling brake system. James Evans had remembered his brief meeting with the mystery cyclist all too well.

The inquest began in earnest at the village hall, Great Glen, on 25 July and after one full day adjourned until 8 August. On the first day the Evans family testified to Bella's arrival at the house in Gaulby and their sighting of the mystery man who arrived with her. Dr Williams reprised his post-mortem evidence and farmer Joseph Cowell retold his story of the discovery of Bella's body. But the most significant and controversial evidence came on the second day when Leicester

Village Hall at Great Glen where the inquest was held. The author

gunsmith, Henry Clarke, took the stand. He had only had a short amount of time to examine the bullet police had found on the day following the shooting and was therefore only able to offer the court a brief and somewhat imprecise evaluation of his findings. Nevertheless according to his testimony the bullet could have been fired from either a revolver or a rifle. If a revolver, which was the weapon favoured by the police, then in his opinion it needed to have been a large one. He told the coroner that his assessment of events was that if the weapon had been fired from close range, say five feet, there would have been scorch marks and powder burns to the face, if from fifty or sixty yards away then the bullet would have passed through the skull. But either way at some point, he claimed, it had struck a hard surface. The indentations on the bullet apparently clearly showed that it must have struck the road or something hard when nearly spent. This meant that the ricochet this caused could have been the cause of the bullet hitting Bella Wright in the head. This caused police to revise, though not necessarily accept, their theory of exactly how the shooting had happened. Up until this point they had always believed that Bella had been shot dead as she rode along the road. A ricochet, they believed, could only have hit her had she been walking, so the revised reconstruction of events tentatively suggested that she had possibly dismounted prior to being hit by the bullet. The problem with this, as they well knew, meant that it compromised the murder theory and replaced it with that of accidental death and that they most certainly did not believe. Nevertheless, they tried to keep an open mind as they widened the search for the stranger and his bicycle, calling in Scotland Yard's best after discovering that a man fitting the circulated description had taken an identical bicycle into Cox's cycle shop on Mere Road, Leicester on the day of the killing for a minor repair.

Believing that this single, key fact, would reveal the mystery man's identity, police were confident of an arrest, but it was a misplaced confidence. Despite a huge manhunt and an increase in the nationwide press coverage that this brought it yielded nothing. Summer turned to winter and by 1 March of 1920 the case was, to all intents and purposes, consigned to the unsolved pile. It was at that juncture that a bargeman on the Leicester canal, whilst attempting to free a towrope, fortuitously dragged a bicycle, minus its back wheel and pedals, to the water's surface. Unaware of the significance of his find he pulled the cycle on board and only handed it to police when his barge had reached Long Eaton, Nottingham. They in turn handed it over to Leicester's Detective Superintendent Taylor simply because it was green in colour. A cursory examination by Leicester police immediately revealed that its identification number had been carefully filed off and suspicions were aroused that this was the cycle everyone had sought throughout the later part of 1919. Taylor then had a stroke of luck. On the top of the front fork, not easily visible because of its position, there was a second, duplicate number, 108678. This took him to the BSA works at Birmingham. The company's sales department were then able to say which of their agents had received the bicycle to sell and that in turn led to its original purchaser, ex-soldier Ronald Light.

Light was arrested in Cheltenham where he worked as an under-master at Cheltenham College, teaching mathematics. A Leicester man by birth, public school educated, he had graduated from the Institution of Civil Engineers with a B.Sc degree in engineering, which had secured him a job with the Midland Railway where he worked until the outbreak of war in 1914. Sent to France at the start of 1915 as an officer with the Royal Engineers, he served until July of that year before resigning his commission in circumstances never fully explained and returned home. Still intent on being involved in the war, he then rejoined the army as a gunner with an artillery company some two months later and was back on the front line by November 1917 where he stayed until August of the following year. Suffering from shell shock he returned initially to Leicester and his parents' home before making the move south. Born in October 1885, described by many as being a bright, intelligent man, he was thirty-four-years-old when Detective Superintendent Taylor finally made the arrest. His arrival back in Leicester on 5 March 1920 on the 11.20 am train went relatively unnoticed.

When questioned at the County Police Station that same day, Light initially claimed never to have owned a green bicycle, refuting the allegation that the bicycle discovered in the canal had been his. Twenty-four hours later, possibly after being confronted with the BSA records from Birmingham, he modified this earlier denial and told police that he had had so many bicycles over the years that he had been confused. The bicycle unearthed from the canal bed he accepted was probably one of these but if so it had been sold some years ago to a man he could no longer recall. It was a pointless attempt to deceive. Police knew when they began the interview that there could be no doubt over ownership. They had already uncovered the ledger from Orton Brothers' bicycle shop,

Ronald Light. Author's collection

Derby, which clearly showed that he had bought the bicycle brand new on 13 May 1910. The bicycle had then been despatched from Birmingham one month later and delivered direct to Light's parents' home in early July. All irrefutable facts, accepted by Light when confronted with them, but facts that only confirmed the bicycle had once been in his possession. It did not prove his was the hand that had cast it into the canal. That hand, Light continued to insist, had belonged to someone else.

Nevertheless, police conviction of his culpability continued to grow. On Monday 7 March 1920 this confidence was reinforced even further when two cycle shop owners were able to clearly identify Light as being the man that brought a green bicycle to their shops during 1919. First, Harry Cox, the man who had claimed days after the murder that Light had brought the machine into his shop on the day of the shooting for a minor repair, made a positive identification when he was confronted with Light at Leicester Police Station. Walter Franks followed this in similar fashion when he told police that his cycle shop on St Stephens Road, Leicester, had been a regular haunt of Light's along with his bicycle during the spring of that same year. The same day police put him into an identity line-up from which key witness, George Measures, Bella's uncle, easily picked him out as the man he had seen waiting in the street for his niece. At that point Light was formally charged with murder.

On 12 March further dredging of the canal brought to the surface an empty revolver holster of the type used by British officers plus twenty-two live rounds of ammunition and seven blanks. Seven days later the rear wheel surfaced and by the end of March police had found the missing pedals, but no gun. Light continued to deny that the bicycle was his and strenuously denied ever owning a revolver. But by late April investigations had revealed that in the case of the latter clear evidence existed to show he had bought a Webley-Scott service revolver in July 1915 from his commanding officer, Major Burton. This revolver had certainly travelled with him to France and, according to a Miss Tunnicliffe, it had been sent back to Leicester in a parcel which she received and which Light had collected from her toward the end of the war. The case against him appeared more air tight the longer time went on.

The trial opened in Leicester on 10 June 1920 before Mr Justice Horridge at 10.30 am. Newspaper reporters had been gathering in the city over the previous two days, such was the demand for news. They in turn had filled all the hotels and the columns of print dedicated to the murder had brought hundreds of people onto the streets. So dense were the crowds that the whole of the Castle Green was covered by people desperate to glimpse a view of Light as he arrived at the court and inside every available space had been filled.

Light, well groomed, smartly dressed in a blue suit and light coloured waistcoat, pleaded not guilty then sat in the dock, elbows resting on the dock rim and watched events unfold. The only certainty he had at that point was the quality of his defence team. During the weeks running up to the trial his family had secured the services of Sir Edward Marshall Hall, the most celebrated defence barrister of his age. Hall, born in 1858, was at the peak of his powers at this time. An orator of outstanding quality whose ability to convince courts that, what he termed as the *invisible weight of the presumption of innocence*, should always tip the scales of justice in favour of the defendant, had won him a number of high profile murder cases. Hall was a consummate actor, feared by prosecutors across the country and loved by both the tabloid press and the public at large. Light must have known that if he was to escape the noose then Hall was his only chance.

But the learned barrister had one severe handicap, his client. There seems little doubt that when the case opened he knew Light had lied. The evidence against him was simply overwhelming. Police had uncovered too many witnesses who placed Light at or around the scene of the crime on the night of the shooting, the bicycle had clearly been in his possession at the time, he had a service record, which meant he knew how to handle a gun and finally he had been known to previously own a revolver of the type believed to have been used in the murder. There was little that could be offered by way of defence once all these factors were brought out into open court, but Light stubbornly refused to change his story and continued to maintain not only his innocence, but also his denial of what were proven facts. When the Attorney General, Sir Gordon Hewitt, got to his feet on day one of the trial and began the prosecution's opening address to the court, the case had all the hallmarks of being a straightforward victory for the crown.

Throughout the morning of that first day a trail of witnesses told the history of the green bicycle, how it had been ordered in Derby, despatched from Birmingham and delivered to Light's home. The family's domestic servant, Mary Webb, recalled how Light had told his mother that he was taking the green bicycle to a different cycle repair shop on the day of the murder, and that before he left the house his mother had told him to be home by 8 pm for a hot supper. She went on to say he had ignored the request and not returned until after ten o'clock, claiming the cycle had broken down. Under further questioning she also recalled that the cycle, after being left in the kitchen was later moved upstairs to a box room, never used again and finally disappeared in December of the same year. When she had enquired as to its whereabouts, she told the court, Light accounted for the cycle's disappearance by claiming he had sold it. She went on to tell the jury the clothes he had worn on the

Newspaper headline of Light's day in court. Leicester Mercury

night of Bella Wright's death had been sold at around the same time. Constable Hall described the discovery of the bullet, where it had been found and its condition and boatman Enoch Whitehouse told the jury how he had accidentally uncovered the bicycle from the depths of Leicester's canal. But the key witness that morning was Henry Clarke.

A partner in the gunsmith firm of Clarke and Sons, Gallowtree Gate, Leicester, he had originally given evidence to the inquest, which by his own admission had been less than precise. Now, having spent a greater amount of time in carrying out the task of examining the spent bullet uncovered at the crime scene, he presented a somewhat different and certainly more detailed assessment of his findings. He told the court he was now certain the bullet had been adapted for use in a service revolver and that the bullet itself was one which had been modified so that it could be used with black powder and cordite. This change had, he explained, come about in 1915 and had been as a result of tests carried out by the military, which showed cordite greatly increased the velocity of the bullet once fired. The ammunition recovered from the canal was of an identical type and all would have been used with a Webley-Scott service revolver. Wounds received by anyone shot using such a weapon and such ammunition would be distinctive in that the entry wound was invariably small but the exit wound much larger depending upon the distance from which the weapon had been fired. In the case of Bella Wright, he told the court the exit wound at the back of her head indicated that the bullet had not lost much of its velocity or else it would have caused less damage, the implication being that whoever fired the shot was not far away from her, possibly no more than six or seven feet (2 metres). The bullet itself had only three marks upon it. One had been caused by a horse, which must have trodden on it as it lay on the road. A second mark had been caused as it exited the dead woman's head and the third as it struck the road. This closer, more detailed examination had caused him to review his earlier conclusion that the killing could have been as a result of a ricochet. Had that been the case he now concluded, there would have been other additional and distinctive characteristics on the bullet, which were clearly not evident.

Marshall Hall attempted under cross examination to show that if the killer had stood as close as six feet (2 metres) the exit wound would have been massive and there would have been powder burns left on the face, therefore the shot must have been fired from some considerable distance and possibly by a rifle, as he had already indicated to the coroner. But the gun-smith was unshakable. The bullet, he told the defence barrister, he was now able to show, had clear rifling marks consistent with having been fired from a revolver. Had a rifle been fired from a greater distance, the exit wound would have been much smaller. He was satisfied that his earlier and inconclusive assessment had been flawed. The wounds sustained by Bella

Wright were, he insisted, compatible with those inflicted by a close range shot and powder burns would not have been evident from six feet (2 metres).

It was damning testimony and during the afternoon session it got worse. When Dr Williams took the stand to repeat his earlier inquest evidence he was far more lucid in his delivery than he had been a year earlier. He had also given a great deal of thought to exactly how Bella Wright had been shot. Although he admitted in court that he had little experience of gunshot wounds he nevertheless offered up a hitherto unheard theory based around his post-mortem findings. The bullet wounds, he told the court, were such that their position in the body offered two possible explanations as to how they had been inflicted. Because of the angle and track of the wound through the brain the first theory, the one favoured by police that suggested she had been riding her cycle, or standing and then shot from close range by someone on her left, was, he agreed, perfectly acceptable except for one fact. The wound had left an upward track through the brain, which meant the shooter was below her line of sight. But, argued the doctor, if this presumed scenario were accurate the bullet would in all likelihood have travelled a far greater distance than the seventeen and a half feet (5.5 metres) it had. If however, Bella had been nearer to the ground when the shot was fired then, and in his opinion only then, would the bullet have travelled a shorter distance. The premise for this conclusion, he told the court, had been based upon the shot travelling upward through the brain but with the victim's head angled in such a way that the bullet would have hit the road surface within feet of exiting the back of the base of the skull: this would have caused a ricochet that would have lessened the distance it then travelled. If this were true then obviously it suggested that Bella Wright had been either pulled or pushed to the ground and the only known person near enough to do that had been Ronald Light. When Sir Edward Marshall Hall left the courtroom at the close of the day there could be little doubt that he knew well enough that if he were to save his client from the gallows he would have to do something remarkable.

When he got to his feet after the Crown had completed its case he called only one witness, the defendant. In all probability there had been some serious debate with Light, either in the days preceding the trial or overnight, and as a result of those conversations there seems little doubt he had been told that his defence was seriously compromised. It was no longer viable to argue that he had not owned the green bicycle at the time of the killing, nor that he had not met Bella on the day of her death. To attempt a defence based around this premise, Marshall Hall knew all too well would lose him the case. So, when Light stood in the witness box on 10 and 11 June before a hushed courtroom and offered up his testimony, it was a revised version of events and a version no one outside the defence team had ever heard before.

After giving his date of birth and some brief background detail he then stunned the court with an admission. Under slow and careful questioning from his defence barrister he told the story of how he had come into the ownership of a Webley-Scott revolver, the holster used to carry it and a quantity of ammunition. The same type of weapon used in the murder. But, according to Light, not the gun that had fired the fatal shot. The gun he had once owned, he insisted, had been lost in an army clearing station at Corby after the war.

Marshall Hall: Had you in your possession at the time (of the murder) any revolver?

Ronald Light: No.

Marshall Hall: Have you ever possessed any revolver except the one you bought from your commanding officer?

Ronald Light: No.

Marshall Hall: Had you any ammunition?

Ronald Light: Yes, between 30 and 40.

Marshall Hall: And were they .45 for the service revolver?

Ronald Light: Yes.

Marshall Hall: And these produced here today were they yours?

Ronald Light: Yes.

It was a startling admission and when he continued in his testimony to confess that it had also been he that had thrown that ammunition, along with the holster into the Leicester Canal there was a ripple of excitement around those sitting in the courtroom. But Marshall Hall had only just begun his defence. Light went on to agree with the prosecution case that he had not only owned a green bicycle but he had taken it out on the evening of 5 July 1919 and that whilst cycling on the road beyond Stoughton had met Annie Bella Wright, though he claimed she was a woman whose name he had not known until he read of her murder in the *Leicester Mercury*.

Marshall Hall: Had you any fixed time in your mind as to the time you intended to return?

Ronald Light: I intended then to get in between eight and half past.

Marshall Hall: Having made that decision did you turn?

Ronald Light: I turned into the road on the right.

Marshall Hall: And in the upper road did you see a young lady riding a bicycle?

Ronald Light: Yes, after I had gone some distance down.

Marshall Hall: Did you know her?

Ronald Light: No.

Marshall Hall: Had you ever seen her before?

Ronald Light: Never.

Another startling admission and they just kept on coming. He told the court how he had cycled alongside her to Gaulby village and how he had waited for her for over an hour. However, according to his story when the two had parted company outside her uncle's house his understanding was that she wanted him to wait. She had not, he insisted, given him the impression that she would be some time inside the house, rather the opposite. But despite this he told the court that after a quarter of an hour he would have cycled off had it not been for the fact he had a slow puncture in the back tyre. It was the repair of this puncture that kept him in Gaulby longer than he had intended and once repaired he saw Bella leaving the house as he cycled past. Stopping, he then went over to her and they spoke briefly, but, he insisted, he did not call her by name. The two then set off again together, though, as Light explained, the puncture he had sustained in the back tyre he had realised at that point he had not repaired properly, which forced him to stop on more than one occasion. When they reached the other side of Kings Norton village, a time he estimated at some ten minutes after leaving Gaulby (probably about 8.45 pm), he left her and cycled off toward Leicester whilst she took the road where her body was later found. He knew no more until he read the lurid headlines in his local paper. This caused him to panic. The killer, according to what he read, was the owner of the green bicycle in his own kitchen and frightened that he would eventually be arrested the bicycle went the same way as the holster, dumped in the canal.

There was a ring of truth to what Light told the court and deciding to change the defence from one of total denial to one of admission, leastways of association, had thrown the prosecution counsel. The Attorney General had returned to London before the defence opened its case, no doubt satisfied he had done enough to convict. The sudden change of tack threw them into a deal of chaos and despite rigorous cross-examination his version of events held up. When Marshall Hall stood up to deliver his closing speech at the end of the trial he must have realised that he was on the verge of achieving one of the most stunning turnarounds in criminal history.

Marshall Hall told the jury that in order to convict they must be satisfied that Light had gone out that day to commit a murder. Furthermore they had to accept that he had decided to kill the first person he met because there was not a single shred of evidence to show that he had ever met Bella Wright before that day. There was no motive, he argued, nothing to offer up a reason why and there was no proof that the bullet found had been the bullet that had killed the young woman. Marshall Hall insisted that the .45 bullet found at the scene could never have inflicted the type of injury Bella Wright had sustained and that the position of the wounds, despite the doctor's theory were inconsistent with a man having fired from close range. Ronald Light, he told them, had done nothing more and nothing less than anyone else in his position would have done. He had simply panicked when he realised that he was being sought for murder, a murder he had not committed and so attempted to destroy the evidence that linked him to the crime. But no one saw him at the crime scene, no one saw him shoot a gun, or heard a bullet fired and no one saw him after the killing. It was a masterful piece of defensive argument and after three hours the jury returned a not guilty verdict. So began one of this country's most baffling and mysterious murders.

Ronald Light died in 1975 aged eighty-nine years and as far as I have been able to ascertain, never discussed the murder in public. There are only three possibilities to the identity of Annie 'Bella' Wright's killer. One was that she was shot accidentally, possibly by someone out shooting birds that night. A whole theory has been raised about a shot being fired from a rifle that killed the crow found near her body and the ricochet then hitting her in the head. But the bird had not been shot, its bloody claw prints showed that it had been alive after the killing, and the wound would never have been so severe had it been a simple ricochet. Two, that some other individual who was never found, had stumbled across Bella and shot her for no other reason than she was there. The third possibility is that she knew her killer and had died as a result of an attack of some sort.

Modern forensic methods would indicate that she was murdered from very close range. Dr Williams told the court that when he had examined Bella's face he had found minute particles of metal around the entry wound but no powder burns. But Constable Hill had also told the court that he had wiped her face clean in his search for the bullet wound. Therefore, there would have been no powder burns to see. But the tiny metal fragments are significant. When a gun is fired there is first a cloud of gas that bursts from the barrel, if the gun barrel is in contact with the skin this would cause a star-like wound. Next, a flame that would cause burning if near to the skin, then the bullet leaves the barrel with a scatter of projectile particles of gunpowder behind it. These blast into the skin around the entry wound causing 'tattooing' and cannot be wiped away. In Bella Wright's case there was no star-like wound and no burning of the skin but there was a spread or tattoo of gunpowder, which is what the doctor probably referred to in his testimony. This means the gun had to have been fired from one to two feet (0.5 metres) away. The grass verge beside the body was nine feet wide. This eliminates the shot being fired accidentally from behind the hedgerow. Whoever shot her stood on that grass verge and Bella definitely knew her killer. Was that Ronald Light? Who knows, so many years later it is difficult to draw conclusions. But he must have been in the vicinity when the gun was fired and if he had not pulled the trigger, as the court believed, ought he not to have heard the shot?

CHAPTER 16

An Unfortunate Affair
The Murder of Nellie Thorpe
1941

She was dead by the time her head hit the ground.

Sixty-one-year-old Thomas Thorpe had been married to the love of his life for over twenty-five years when the war started and, by May 1940, he had begun to realise that his marriage was in serious jeopardy. There were tell-tale signs that suggested Nellie, his wife, had begun to meet with another man. At that stage Thomas had no idea who the man was but recognised the signs easily enough. She, of course, denied the accusation, but the damage had been done and the steady marriage that had endured so long began to break apart. By January 1941 the arguments had become more frequent and serious in nature. Thomas had discovered, probably through friends and neighbours, that Nellie had become involved with a man named Scrimshaw, though she continued with her denials. This in turn had led to an escalation in the nature of their fights and Thomas had begun to exhibit a violent streak Nellie would never have believed he could have possessed. This eventually forced her to seek sanctuary amongst her friends and at the beginning of March she left the marital home and began to lodge with Elizabeth Parsons. The two women had known each other for a number of years; both worked at the nearby shoe factory, and had often walked home together. Elizabeth, some twenty-three years Nellie's junior, had been a regular witness to some of these arguments and despite the age difference was happy enough to take Nellie in. Just how much she knew of the secret liaison between Nellie and her new man is not known but easily imagined.

Leicester Infirmary. The author

Thomas, distraught by the sudden break-up of his marriage, took poison. Though it is doubtful he had any intention of dying as a result, probably rather the opposite. Desperate to win his wife back he no doubt hoped that an attempt at suicide would be seen as a cry for help, an appeal possibly to his wife's compassionate nature. Needless to say he survived and after a short stay at Leicester Infirmary returned home. Nellie, as far as is recorded, stayed away. For the despondent Thomas, this brush with death was then compounded by news that he had lost his job. This meant he could no longer pay his rent and he was forced to leave his home on Welford Road. Some of the household furniture was sold and it was left to his married daughter, Nellie Porteous, to take him in. All too well aware of what had been happening to her parents and with a spare bedroom to let, there was probably little alternative, although Thomas still believed the move was to be temporary. Harbouring the hope that life could be returned to what he saw as normality, he then embarked upon a plan to rebuild his marriage. The plan was simple enough. He would set up a series of meetings with his wife over the course of the spring and attempt to convince her that they could rebuild their relationship. But Nellie was having none of it.

Spring turned to summer and Thomas's attempts at gentle persuasion began to take on a more sinister edge. Determined that she would see the error of her ways, and by now ever more desperate to convince her that a return to a new family home was the only acceptable solution to their problems, he became more physical. The meetings, which had understandably become less frequent as the months went by, were marred by an increase in violence whenever they did take place. Consumed by anger and unable any longer to contain the frustration he obviously felt each and every time his attempts at reconciliation failed, he turned to an almost predictable level of violence.

Nellie was attacked on a number of occasions throughout the summer months of 1941. Some of these attacks amounted to no more than being pushed or shouted at, others were more serious with most being witnessed by other people. But probably the worst of these was an attempt to strangle her to death outside the factory where she worked. Incensed by what he saw as Nellie's unwarranted intransigence toward him each and every time the two met, he had completely lost control after yet another failure at reconciliation and she was possibly only saved by the timely intervention of a number of her work friends. But for whatever reason, she refused to call in the police. It was a mistake she would pay dearly for.

On 14 July Thomas, who had by this time left his daughter's house and taken up lodgings, resigned himself to murder. Leaving the house in the early evening he made his way to Nellie's place of work, timing the journey so that he would arrive just as she finished her shift. At a little after 5.30 pm he stood and watched as she, Elizabeth Parsons and a young

Abbey Street, Leicester. The author

woman named Sarah Carr, made their way out through the factory gates and into Abbey Street. Unseen by any of the three he attacked from behind, caught Nellie by the neck, forced her to the ground and slit her throat with a cut-throat razor. She was dead by the time her head hit the ground. Then, in full view of a street full of witnesses he slashed the blade across his own neck. Unfortunately for Thomas, like the attempt at poisoning some months earlier, it was a half-hearted attempt at killing himself and he was easily wrestled to the ground by a passing cyclist. There was never going to be any doubting his guilt and if any motive were needed, he was only too willing to provide it. In front of the gathered crowd he looked down at the prostrate body of his, by now, dying wife and with venom told her, 'I'll give you going about with other men'.

He continued to condemn himself after being arrested, telling Detective Superintendent Ashburner, whilst the two men stood on the street watching a medical team making a failed attempt to save Nellie's life, that he had killed her because she had refused to end her long-running affair, insisting that he loved her so much that he was not going to allow any other man into her life:

> *She's been standing in with another man for twelve months. She's admitted it to me. She's been the best woman in the world. I love her that much that I'll see no other man has her.*

It was a statement that he must have known was going to condemn him.

When the trial opened before Mr Justice Stable on 29 October twelve weeks incarcerated in prison had brought about not only a change in attitude, but also a change of view when it came to his own involvement in the murder. All too well aware that he had said far too much after his arrest, and needing to mitigate his culpability as far as he was able, he set about weaving a story around the murder intending to show that his actions had been accidental. He told the court that he had never intended harm to his wife. When he saw her leaving work on the day of the murder he claimed he had only intended to frighten her. The cut-throat razor, he insisted, he had drawn from its sheath but with the blunt side uppermost. The intention had been to run this blunt side across her throat, thereby causing no injury. The death had been unintentional and, according to his own testimony, it had been Nellie's left hand, raised in self-defence that had hit the razor turning it over on to its sharp side that had caused him to cut her throat:

> I didn't make my mind up 'till four yards away from my wife, and then I suddenly thought I'd play a joke on her as I have done that same thing on myself many a time when I've been shaving – to draw the back of the razor across my own throat and say, "There goes nothing." I've shouted at the missus out of the kitchen to see me do it and she has said. "You fool." That's what I was going to do – to draw the back of the razor across her throat to frighten her and make her come back. I got behind her, she never saw me, I stood at the back of her, put my left arm around her neck with my left hand underneath her chin. I had tried the razor on the back of my hand to see that I'd got the blunt end. As I was nearing her throat with the back of the razor – the razor was loose in my right hand – she brought her left hand up and hit the sharp edge of the razor with the back of her hand and must have turned it over, but I did not feel it move. In the excitement I drawed it across her throat. I was amazed to see blood spout onto my right hand . . .

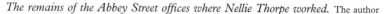

The remains of the Abbey Street offices where Nellie Thorpe worked. The author

It was certainly a different slant on events compared to how they had seemed when police had made the initial arrest. Unfortunately for Thomas medical evidence did not appear to support his statement. According to the post-mortem results presented in court there were no other wounds, other than those on the throat, that corresponded with this version. The left hand, which he insisted had knocked the blade over, sustained no corroborative injuries, which was unlikely, given the sharpness of the blade and the fact that there had been two cuts on Nellie's throat was suggestive of a deliberate action. If, as Thomas had argued, the attack had simply been a joke gone wrong, then it were likely only one wound, a sweeping cut, would have been made. The two cuts she sustained had both been serious, one to the left of her neck some one and a half inches long, the other on the right some five inches long, which left little doubt that the attack had been pressed home with some force and that the attacker had intended to kill.

In his summing up the judge pointed out that whilst it may seem a reasonable defence to argue that the attack had not been an attempt to kill but to frighten, no mention had been made by Thomas either at the time of his arrest or during his three months in prison. This, he suggested, was certainly suspicious particularly when taken into account alongside the statement he had made at the scene of the killing. The jury agreed and after a short adjournment returned an expected guilty verdict with a recommendation to mercy.

None was forthcoming and Thomas William Thorpe was duly executed at Leicester on Tuesday 23 December 1941, by Thomas and Albert Pierrepoint.

High Street, Leicester, c.1920. Author's collection

CHAPTER 17

All For The Sake of Love The Murder of Nora Emily Payne 1944

... he had travelled that day from Norwich with only one clear intention ...

When Nora Payne met Norwich painter William Cowle just after the outbreak of the war she was swept off her feet. Cowle had a charming, easy personality, which appealed to her and by the start of 1941 he had moved from Norwich to Leicester and taken up lodgings in Saxby Street. His landlady, Nellie Jones, knew nothing of the blossoming relationship when he took up the rent and, despite being ever vigilant when it came to her lodgers' sexual appetites, never saw Nora at the house throughout his stay, which lasted almost until the year end. What she did know though disturbed her greatly. The more she saw of her lodger the more she began to realise that he was a manic depressive, prone on occasion to bouts of crying that sometimes lasted all day and always armed with a knife, something he had carried since being attacked in the street in 1938. Whether Nora was aware of this character flaw and Cowle's tendency to carry a weapon is not known

Saxby Street, Leicester. The author

but it would appear not. Either way, if she was aware it appears not to have caused her any concerns because the relationship continued to strengthen.

Perhaps, if she had known more about the man she initially found so appealing, the relationship between herself and the young house painter would have remained amicable but far less intense. As it was Nora, it would appear, never discovered the detail behind Cowle's life that made him such a complex character. Born in Liverpool where he had continued to live until just after his twenty-first birthday, Cowle had left the city in 1934, driven by a desire to travel around the country. This had meant, much to the consternation of his own family, that he abandoned any notion of settling into a trade, developing a skill and creating the sense of stability that parents crave for their children. Instead, he became an itinerant worker taking odd jobs where he could find them and living, at times, in lodgings they would never have approved of. At some point toward the end of the 1930s, surprisingly to those that knew him, he also married. The marriage was short, never happy and for the most part somewhat unstable. It was also a marriage Nora was never to know about despite the fact Cowle and his wife never divorced. Whether the break-up took him to Norwich or whether he just arrived there on one of his travels, is not known but certainly he found work there and stayed working in or around the city until the end of 1940 when he came to Leicester.

He and Nora met at some point around this time and the year he spent on Saxby Street was probably the most successful year as far as their relationship went. Nora, twenty eight years old when the two met, was working as a clerk at the offices of the Petroleum Board in Leicester. She had worked there since leaving school and there is nothing to suggest she was ever anything other than happy in her job. Surrounded by friends, and with an active social life, it is doubtful that she would ever have given Cowle more than a passing glance had he not been persistent. Exhibiting no signs of the depression that haunted him when they met, she initially found his company stimulating, possibly enthralled by his stories of years on the road and almost certainly flattered by the attention he paid her.

The relationship deepened, though there is nothing to suggest that they were ever lovers. But pressures created by the war began to have a detrimental effect. When Cowle left his lodgings on Saxby Street it was to join the army and the two parted for the first time. Throughout the next year they wrote to each other on a regular basis and for Cowle it was the love affair he had sought for most of his life. If Nora had been able to reciprocate then quite possibly events would have turned out very differently. But for her, there was no passionate affair and the feelings she had initially held for the young house painter began to cool. When he returned to civilian life in June of 1943 after being invalided out of his regiment it was to find that the love of his life had turned away from him and was looking to put an end to the brief relationship. By this time back in Norwich, he doggedly resisted her attempts to push him away and the two somehow managed to stay together, albeit at a distance, for another nine months. But in May of 1944 Nora had finally had enough and wrote to Cowle finally calling a halt:

> *It is not my fault that fate plans life a different way. Don't come to Leicester. I shall be cross. More than that I shall not see you ... I have never written a letter like this before and I hope I never shall again ... I will wish you good health and place you in the safe keeping of our heavenly father ...*

On Thursday 18 May, Cowle purchased a train ticket at Norwich station and travelled into Leicester. He met with Nora at around midday and the meeting was fraught. Nora had not expected Cowle to make the long journey, no doubt having presumed the letter would be sufficient to end their affair without having a final confrontation. But Cowle had never been likely to accept the situation without there being a meeting of some sort. He had timed the train journey so he would arrive at Leicester railway station with sufficient time for him to walk to her home and meet her as she made the short walk back to work after her lunch. Whether or not Nora was shocked at finding him in the street when she left for the office is, of course, not known, but certainly it was unlikely that she would have been afraid of him. Cowle had exhibited no signs of violence

Springfield Road where Nora Payne was murdered. The author

throughout their long association, nor had he ever raised his voice in anger. So, when the two met, she was no doubt understandably anxious at being suddenly confronted, but nevertheless readily agreed to walk a while and explain the reasons behind her letter. The two walked to Springfield Road, Leicester, not far from where she was living, and there stepped into the shadow of a narrow entry. They talked a little more in the privacy of the passageway then Cowle, by now realising the futility of his attempt at reconciliation, took her in his arms and in a farewell embrace kissed her. The relationship was finally at an end. But for Nora, as she shared in that final emotional embrace, there was to be no escape. As Cowle stepped away from her he drew a knife from his pocket and stabbed her in the neck. He then ran out into the street, paused a moment, then ran back into the entry and stabbed her four more times before running off. Nora, by now mortally wounded, managed to drag herself out into the middle of the road, blood pouring from her throat and neck. Ivy Laurie, who lived in the same street and had witnessed the attack, ran to her aid. Nora died an hour or so later. Meanwhile Cowle, who had no intention of escape, surrendered himself to the first policeman he saw.

From the moment of his arrest it became clear that he had travelled that day from Norwich with only one clear intention,

The Belmont House Hotel *where Cowle left the letters.* The author

to murder Nora Payne. He told police that he had killed her because she had deliberately ended their affair. He also told them that he had left a suitcase behind the clock at the *Belmont House Hotel,* De Montfort Street, which contained a number of love letters including the final letter from Nora and had thrown the murder weapon into a garden. Both were quickly recovered and Cowle was charged with murder.

The trial, which took place in Nottingham in order to allow the defence more time, opened some six weeks later, on 26 June. In the interim the defence team, despite the mounting evidence being collated against their client, began to put Cowle through a series of rigorous mental examinations. With no doubt as to his guilt the only strategy available to them was one of mental incapacity. Cowle, they would argue, was insane at the time he committed the murder. There were good grounds for mounting this type of defence. Cowle had clearly been a depressive for much of his life and had exhibited clear signs of some sort of mental decline over the previous four or five years. The tearful breakdowns at his lodgings throughout 1941 were used as proof positive that he had suffered some sort of mental collapse whilst in the relationship with Nora. Both his mother and brother-in-law also testified in court that since leaving home he had begun to collect useless items of everyday life;

nails, bits of string, seashells and old socks with no feet in them. All these he had apparently kept in a suitcase or sometimes in his jacket pockets. He had complained of headaches or pains in his head, had often been emotional for no reason and had been taking tablets to help him sleep. The medical officer at Leicester Prison told the court that in his opinion all these incidents were signs of mental collapse:

Having regard to what I have seen and heard in conversation, I formed the opinion that he was suffering from mental disease on May 18. He had periods of depression, lasting sometimes for three days, and at these times he talked about suicide. There have been other periods of time in between when he seemed comparatively happy. He would say then that he was free from worry and when I asked him he would say: I can't remember anything about it. What is there to worry about. On these occasions he had written lengthy chatty letters to his friends, not such letters as would be expected from a man in his position. He had also written several pieces of verse.

The doctor went on to express an opinion that William Cowle was suffering from manic depressive insanity and would never have understood the nature or quality of the murder he had committed at the time he was carrying it out. The final letter from Nora, he went on, would have acted as a catalyst that would have unbalanced his fragile mental state and precipitated the killing.

A second examination carried out by a Dr Colahan on 21 June, five days before the trial, concurred and added that in his opinion Cowle would only have realised he had committed murder when he saw blood on his own hands. According to this additional corroborative testimony he had only one recollection of the events of 18 May and that was; 'Kissing Miss Payne'.

Police Headquarters, Leicester c.1940. Author's collection

Powerful stuff – and clearly a strong defence argument in favour of Cowle's unbalanced mind being the cause of his actions and not premeditation – but not supported by the prosecution's only medical witness, Birmingham medical officer, John Humphrey. He had spent two hours with Cowle three weeks earlier and did not share the views of the two defence doctors. In his opinion Cowle was sane and certainly knew what he had done. During his interview, he told the court, the defendant had given him a clear and coherent account of his life up to and including the day of his arrest. Furthermore, he had a clear recollection of events and in the medical officer's opinion was far from insane.

It was a piece of testimony that wrecked the whole defence case. After an adjournment of fifty-five minutes the jury returned a verdict of guilty. Mr Justice Singleton then sentenced him to death. He was executed at Leicester in February alongside William Meffen, who had murdered his stepdaughter at Chaddesden, Derby, in the first double execution at Leicester prison for forty-one years.

CHAPTER 18

Killed to See How it Felt
The Murder of Janet Warner
1953

... he never suspected anything untoward had happened to his daughter.

When Walter Warner saw the family dog, Rex, crawl through a hole in the fence at the bottom of his garden at a little after six-thirty in the evening, he never suspected that anything untoward had happened to his daughter. He just thought that she had gone to take care of a friend's horse, as she had done on many an occasion before, and sent the dog home without her. It had become a regular habit for her to take the little black and white dog for a walk every day at around 6 pm. May had been a particularly good month and with temperatures topping a record 80 degrees during the day he thought it more than likely that she had decided to go on to friends rather than return home. Believing his daughter to be safe and having promised to drop his wife and her sister off at the Odeon cinema later that evening he decided to leave her wherever she was until he got back, which was at a little after 8 pm. Half an hour later police were knocking at his door to tell him she had been found dead.

At about a quarter-past six that same evening, three young schoolboys heard a girl screaming on the edge of the Lady Rollestone Spinney near to a place beside the canal at Aylestone, known as Blue Bank. As they ran toward the source of the screams they saw a man stooping over the body of a young girl. When he saw the boys he ran away and disappeared into the wood. The girl, twelve-year-old Janet Warner, was dead when they found her. She had been strangled to death with a woman's nylon stocking and a green tie. For two hours her identity remained a mystery until the tie, a part of her South Wigston Secondary Modern school uniform, led police first to the school and then to the Warner home on Leicester Road, Glenhills and her patiently waiting father.

Within hours police were circulating a description of the man with untidy black hair, believed to have a broken nose and wearing a pair of blue-grey overalls that came up high under his

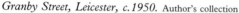
Granby Street, Leicester, c.1950. Author's collection

chin. A mobile crime unit was set up near to the crime scene and a ground search involving hundreds of police, Special Constables, tracker dogs from the army depot at Melton Mowbray and scores of local people went on throughout the night. All main roads were closed down within a radius of thirty miles, roadblocks put in place, a light plane brought in to fly across the open landscape in search of any lone figure and railway stations monitored for anyone fitting the description. On the following day, Monday 23 May, with temperatures soaring to 85 degrees, police began a house-to-house enquiry that eventually made the breakthrough and led them to the door of John Christopher Reynolds.

A thirty-one-year-old softly-spoken Irishman, Dublin-born Reynolds had arrived in England in 1943. Educated at a convent school for the first ten years of his life, he had completed that education at a Christian Brothers School in Southern Ireland. He joined the army in Eire at the outbreak of the Second World War but had been discharged after seven months and had decided instead to join the RAF, which is why he had arrived on the mainland. At the end of the war he had decided not to return to Ireland and after an uncertain period had arrived in Leicester. When police found him he was lodging in a house on Uppingham Road, Leicester, where he had been living for several months. Polite, outwardly shy, he rarely drank

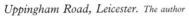

Uppingham Road, Leicester. The author

and was considered by those that knew him to be a loner. He
had few friends but those he did have knew him to be opposite
of what the police believed when they first arrived at his landlady's front door. But Reynolds, as the world was to discover,
was a Jekyll and Hyde character and the man everyone believed
him to be was founded upon a lie. He made no attempt at
denial, acknowledging his guilt from the first interview he had
with the investigating police team. As far as he was concerned
he had wanted to be caught and had no intention of ever
denying the murder.

At his first appearance before Leicester magistrates on
22 June Detective Superintendent Lacy read out to the court
a statement he had made shortly after his arrest:

*For the past ten days or so I have had a feeling to kill somebody. I
waited my chance along the canal at Aylestone. At first I was
going to kill a man who used to go past at a certain hour every day
but the day that I killed Janet he did not come that way. I was just
leaving when I saw the girl coming through the wood with a dog. I
suggested that we go rabbitting. When in the bushes I caught hold
of her. She began to scream so I beat her with my hands and feet. I
had a mixture of feelings. But I could not stop. I saw the stocking
with which I meant to strangle her lying on the ground. I picked it
up and tied it round her neck to make sure she was dead. The girl
was very brave in the face of death. I hope when my time comes I
will be half as brave.*

He was ordered to take his trial at the autumn assizes; that trial
opened on 26 October before Mr Justice Pilcher. Despite
strenuous attempts to force Reynolds to change his guilty
stance and allow a defence team to mount a case of insanity, he
refused. Declaring that he deserved to die for the murder he
had committed, he stood in front of a packed courtroom and an
all male jury, after having been vilified on his arrival by the huge
crowds that had gathered around the courthouse, and pleaded
guilty. Looking calm in a blue double breasted suit, wearing an
open-neck, white shirt and clean shaven, he stood with head
bowed in silent prayer as the judge had the black cap placed

Headline of the Reynolds trial. Leicester Mercury

upon his head and passed the sentence of death. He then turned on his heel and was led down to the cells. The whole thing had only lasted four minutes.

On Tuesday 17 November 1953 Albert Pierrepoint executed him at Leicester prison. Doubtless his death was much quicker than that of his young victim.

Index